Envy

THAT BROOKLYN CHICK

BY

ESHA JAY

By Tyiesha P Johnson

Published 2016

ISBN 13: 978-0-692-79626-9

Cover Design – Kreationsk.com

Additional copies of this book may be obtained by sending an email to:

BLACKMOGULINC@GMAIL.COM

Dedicated

To My Brother Jemal "Get Back" Johnson, (6/16/1980 – 7/23/2003) "Loved by few, hated by many but respected by all!"

Acknowledgment

First I want to thank GOD, for my life, my health, and my strength. And also, for granting me the opportunity to tell my story.

Shout out to Stacey "BO" Knight, my partner for believing in me, standing by me and assisting me with following my dreams. I would also like to shout out my mother, Jessica Johnson, who always supports and believes in me. I'd also like to acknowledge my dad Sincere for standing by me, giving me inspiration, strength and motivation. A special shout out to my young soldiers, Tymel and Sundiata, and my two brothers, Stavon and Trevon. Author Teri Woods, Author Kawand Crawford, My designer Nicole Shephard, James "Jesse James" Graham, along with my family and friends and all of you that supported and continued to support me through my journey. Thank you all and God bless!

Preface

In the many different places that I have been, I've heard so many different stories about NY. Nine out of ten, it's from someone who has never stepped foot in the City. You can't tell a true story about an experience that you never had or a place that you've never been. So I made it my business to take readers on a journey into the world of N.Y.C, for real for real.

Brooklyn raised me! Brooklyn also made me into the independent, smart woman I have become. The credit goes to my loving mother's grounded rules, morals and support. I am also the woman I am because I listened to my big brother who, before his untimely death, encouraged me to always speak my mind and aim for the stars while fighting off the haters. He encouraged me to be a go-getter and not settle. And last but not least, I am who I am from my father teaching me about respect, character, courage and how to be strong when faced with adversity.

I'm a beast and no matter where I go, there will always be a Brooklyn chick in me.

-Tyiesha P. Johnson

Intro

NOW THE DAY HAS COME…

July 23rd, 2003 was the day that Envy, a chick from Brooklyn, Bed-Stuy to be exact, had always dreaded to see. It was 10 minutes after one in the afternoon and Envy, a feisty 21-year-old, was asleep when the phone began ringing.

Ring, Ring, Ring…

The phone must've sounded off about six times before anyone answered it. Envy didn't bother to answer it because there was a full house at her Aunt Jasmine's apartment, which was where she was staying for the time being. Envy knew that one of her four cousins would eventually answer the phone.

There was Chelsea, waiting on her baby father to call from Rikers Island, a prison located in Queens, Ciara was starving for her new shawty to call and their two little bad ass brothers, Leon and Nashawn, were lingering around. With her peeps milling around the house, Envy was not about to jump up out of her sleep to answer the phone.

Eventually, the ringing stopped and about two minutes later, Ciara entered the room where Envy was resting.

"Envy, are you woke? It's your friend Dee Dee," she stated, standing in the doorway while holding the phone in her left hand with the other hand on her hip.

"Tell her that I'm resting. I'll hit her back later," Envy snarled at her cousin.

Ciara sucked her teeth and sighed out loud before placing the phone back to her ear. "Dee Dee, Envy is sleep and ain't tryna get up. Do you wanna leave a message or call her back around 2:30?" CiCi asked, relaying Envy's message before speaking again. "Envy, she said that it's important. She needs to speak to you, NOW!"

Envy, with a Gucci scarf wrapped around her hair and her eyes closed, was thinking that Dee Dee wanted to tell her some gossip. Envy thought it was about what chick wanted to holla at Black, Envy's baby's father, or she wanted to smoke some bud. Envy was reluctant to answer because her newborn had kept her up all night.

"CiCi, ask her what, man. Ima call her back, DAMN!" Envy whined with her eyes still closed. She was not about to allow anyone to disturb her rest, especially while the baby was finally asleep.

"Dee Dee, she said that she'll call you back," CiCi repeated but Dee Dee would not be deterred. "Envy, here. Take the phone. She keeps saying that she really need to holla at you and I'm not about to stand here and go back and forth with the messages," CiCi complained as she walked over to the bed and passed Envy the phone.

"What up, Dee Dee? What's poppin'?" Envy questioned, barely moving a muscle.

"Yooo, son, whatchu doing?" Dee Dee quickly spoke with concern in her voice.

"Nothing much, I was knocked out. A chick is finally able to get some rest from this baby hollering all night. What's so important that it can't wait till later?" Envy wanted to know.

As humble as Envy was, Dee Dee did not want to disturb her mood or spirit but she also knew that she had to tell Envy something that she was not ready to hear. Dee Dee took a deep breath before spitting it out as fast and as clear as possible, "Your brother just got shot in the head!"

Envy opened her eyes, sat up on the bed and quickly responded, “My who? My what? What are you talking about?”

“Envy, it’s Jah! They said that he’s lying on the ground right now on the corner of Putnam and Marcus Garvey!”

“OH MY GOD! You’re lying. Not my brother! Noooo, is he alive?” she responded, confused while scratching her head through her scarf.

“Yea, son. they said he’s still outside on the ground waiting for the ambulance. I’m about to go around there now!” Dee Dee frantically explained what little she knew.

Envy began to panic because she’d just had a premonition the night before that her brother got killed by his homies and how they’d plotted to get rid of him. Most of them were afraid of her brother.

Envy pictured herself at his funeral rubbing his chest while he was in his all-white casket. Therefore, when Dee Dee gave her the news, it was like “Now the day has come!”

Chapter 1

7 YEARS EARLIER

It was 1996, mid-June, Envy and her brother Jah were sitting on the living room sofa in their Gates Avenue apartment scheming on how to escape their mother's watching eye for the weekend.

"Jah, what you doing this weekend?" Envy asked while brushing her beautiful, shoulder length, jet black hair.

"I don't know. I wanna go to St Marks because it's a party in Albany PJs tonight," he responded.

"I wish I could go, but I know that Mommy is not going to let me," Envy whined.

"Even if Mommy said that you can go, you won't be at the party with me!" Jah said as he got as close as possible and yelled in Envy's face. "YOU'RE NOT GOING WITH ME!" Then he burst out laughing.

"That isn't fair! Envy complained.

"You're my little sister and you're only 14. Why would I let you party with me?" Jah asked. Jah was only two years older than Envy but acted like her father. "You shouldn't wanna party with me anyway, cause you ain't dubbing with nobody! None of them Albany boys will be grinding on my little sister. Not tonight," Jah spoke firmly.

"Ain't nobody thinking about them, so what are you talking about? But anyway, we should clean up so that when Mommy comes, she can let us go out. I got the kitchen and you get the living room," Envy rationed out chores before heading to the kitchen and Jah agreed.

By the time Mercedes reached home, the apartment was spotless.

"Oh gosh! Who came through here and cleaned up like this? God must've sent me an angel," Mercedes joked when entering the house after her initial shock of how clean it was. "HEY, YAL! WHAT ARE YAL UP TO!?" Mercedes screamed as she examined the place.

"NOTHING MUCH, MA. WE JUST WANTED TO CLEAN UP FOR YOU!" Envy yelled from hcr room.

"I think yal want something. Since when do yal just clean up without me having to tell yal; and especially this good? Mercedes questioned knowing her children.

"No, Ma. We just wanted to surprise you. I cleaned the living room and Envy cleaned the kitchen." Jah gave his mother a hug and lied through his teeth, as usual, because Envy had cleaned everything by herself while Jah went out in the staircase and smoked his blunt.

"Okay, good. Since yal don't want anything, go and get ready for church."

"Ma, I don't know what Envy is talking about, but I do want something. I wanna go to St Marks. Please, Ma, can I go? Jah pleaded.

"Tonight is service. It's a known fact before you go anywhere on Friday nights, we must go to church together. After nine, you can leave," Mercedes explained.

"What about me, Ma? Can I go?" Envy asked after entering the living room where her mother and brother were.

"No, Envy. You know I'm not sending you nowhere without me."

"But Ma, why can't I spend the night with Aunt Beverly and Dora? Envy asked.

"I'm not sending you over there without any supervision so you can sneak to the projects. I know that's where Dora hangs out every day and come in when she feels like it. She waits till her mother is full of Private Stock beer and once Beverly falls asleep, she make her move and stays out all night. So do you really think that I'm about to send you out there? Not at all, girl! With that being said, how was school today?"

Jah answered first with his lie, "School was aiight, Ma, but I almost got into a fight. This dude came walking up to me, talking about I owe him some money for his Walkman. I told him that I didn't touch his Walkman, it was another dude that he let hold it. He started breaking on me when his crew came around. But when I dropped my books, the security guard came so we ran." Jah had just told the biggest lie knowing that he never stepped foot in school today.

Mercedes knew that Jah was lying, but she decided to feed into his story just to shake him up a little bit. "I need to come up to that school Monday. This is nonsense that you can't get an education because people want to accuse you of taking their stuff."

"No, Ma! You don't have to because we didn't fight or get caught so the school doesn't know what happened," Jah tried to cover his lie.

"Yal didn't fight this time but what if it would have escalated to a fight? Then you would have gotten suspended, all for something that you didn't do. Why did he think that you took it, anyway?" Mercedes asked.

"He let me listen to it in the lunchroom the other day and I gave it back to him when I got done but he forgot where he put it. So he tried to act like I never gave it back to him," Jah's lie grew even bigger.

"See, that's what I'm talking about. You can't get the proper education if you have people harassing you about a bunch of nonsense." Mercedes knew that Jah was lying but didn't know to what extent. She knew eventually it will come out. "Okay, Jah, I'm going to deal with that later. Envy, how was your day?"

"My day was good. They let us stay outside longer today being that the weather was nice until somebody pulled the fire alarm and Mr. Cummings made everyone come inside. Other than that, school was cool," Envy explained.

Mr. Cummings, aka BBC (Bad Breath Cummings), was the principal at J.H.S 324. Envy didn't care about having to go back in school early as long as she saw her junior high sweetie, David, a light skinned, bowlegged guy with green eyes that most of the girls liked.

"It's good to see that not everyone had a bad day. Mine was good, too," Mercedes said. "Being that the house is clean, we can go ahead and get ready for church," Mercedes instructed before Envy and Jah went to get ready.

After the three of them prepared for church, they left.

"It's nice outside so we can walk theses three blocks," Mercedes suggested once they were outside.

"Ma, I don't feel like walking. Oh, my gosh! (OMG wasn't out then)," Envy stated as she sucked her teeth.

"Gates and Malcolm X Boulevard is only three blocks. You walk them same blocks every day for school, so please save it," Mercedes snapped back.

Envy's brother Jah put his two cents in it, "I know, right? It's not that far to walk, with your black self. You like walking down there anyway to see that light skinned dude. What's his name, Ma?" Jah asked as he smirked at Envy, obviously picking at her dark skinned complexion.

"Shut up, Jah! You need to mind your business before I tell on you," Envy threatened as she rolled her eyes.

"Yea, his name is David! Let me catch her sneaking down to Malcolm X to see him. Ima beat her right in front of David," Mercedes spoke out loud, making her position known.

"And Envy don't have nothing to tell on me Ma. She's just making that up," Jah said, defending himself.

"Envy, what are you talking about?" Mercedes finally asked while they strolled up Gates Avenue.

Envy thought about telling on Jah because he was trying to put her on blast but, as usual, she lied because she never wanted Jah to get in trouble. "Nothing, Ma. I was just making that up because he was making me mad. But I really don't have anything to tell on him," Envy covered for her big brother.

"Yea, right. He did something that you know about but that's okay. You don't have to tell it. But if I find out that he did something and you knew about it, then you're getting into trouble right along with him," Mercedes made clear.

Envy wasn't worried at all, although she did know that Jah was smoking weed in the hallway earlier before Mercedes got home. She also knew that he'd cut school and chilled with Corey, his best friend. How would Mercedes ever find out that Envy knew that? She wasn't with him and Jah sure wasn't going to tell it, being that Envy didn't blow him up. If Mercedes ever found out, Jah wouldn't mention Envy's name anyway.

Before they realized it, they were already on Gates and Malcolm X Boulevard. The huge church was directly on the corner. They stopped at the store to grab some Tic Tacs and peppermints before going in. For some reason, some people in church had the most stink breath. They would talk directly in your face with the worst breath in the world! Being a child, what can you do other than suck it up and smell it? There was never any disrespect towards the elders of the church.

Once they entered the church, they took their seats and joined the service that was already going on. Church was usually live on Friday nights because it was a service for the youth. The ceremony was to keep kids off of the streets. There was plenty of singing, dancing and shouting of the Word, which everyone enjoyed.

At exactly 9:30 on the dot, Jah was on it. "Ma, can I leave now?"

"What time is it?" Mercedes was so in tuned with God that she hadn't realized how quickly time had passed.

"It's 9:30!" Jah quickly answered.

"Go ahead, and you better be home by 11:30," she answered.

"I need bus fare to get there and back."

Mercedes gave Jah $10 and sent him on his way. Shortly after Jah left, service was over. Mercedes did her usual, talk to every member of the church, both young and old. Envy greeted the older ones and chatted with the younger members as well. Mercedes would never stop talking. Everyone was leaving and she was still finding people to talk to.

"Maaaaa, come on," Envy finally whined in aggravation.

"Don't rush me, little girl. I'm coming. Okay sister let me go. I'll call you later," Mercedes concluded with one of the elders.

Mercedes and Envy walked around the corner to the Chinese restaurant on Quincy and Malcolm X. They sold the best shrimp and broccoli in the hood. They ordered their food and about 10 minutes later, it was ready. Instead of walking home, they took the 52 bus that ran up Gates Ave, the short distance to the house.

Mercedes and Envy made it home, got comfortable and ate their food before the phone began ringing.

RING, RING, RING…

"Envy, answer that!"

RING, RING, RII…

"Hello." Envy picked up the phone.

"Hey, Envy, where is your mother?" Stacy asked.

Stacey was Mercedes' first cousin and they were close like sisters. They were so close that even their baby fathers Sin and Marvin were brothers. Sin was Envy's father.

"Hold on, Stacey. Ma, it's Stacey," Envy said as she passed her mother the phone.

"Hey, girl, wassup?" Mercedes asked while chewing on a mouthful of food.

"Nothing much, girl! We're down here in Marcy playing cards."

"Oh really! I didn't know that it was a game tonight," Mercedes responded excitedly.

"Yea, well, you better come on if you want a seat because everybody didn't get here yet," Stacey said, encouraging Mercedes to come to the game.

"Okay, girl. I'm on my way. I'll see you in a minute," Mercedes stated before hanging up the phone. "Envy, get ready. We're going to Marcy for a little while."

That was right up Envy's alley. There was a party in Tompkins Projects that had been promoted around school all day and there was a party in Albany Projects. Both places were Envy's stomping grounds. She knew that with Mercedes and 'em playing cards, it would be easy for her to sneak out. The loud music and the noisy people would distract Mercedes and make going to Tompkins easier for Envy.

Envy made sure she put on one of her best outfits. She quickly took off the cute skirt she had worn to church and changed into her red and gray Iceberg spandex sweat suit with her matching red and gray Air Max 95s. Envy bumped her hair to add a lil bend and volume to it, glossed her lips, and put on most of her mother's jewelry. She wrapped her hair and tied it down until it was time to leave.

Mercedes did her little flip mode from "Church Lady" to "Sissy." Sissy was her other name that some of her family members called her. She threw on her jean suit, her navy blue boots and switched from her church glasses to her thin gold frames. Mercedes then added some jewelry accessories to go with it, all that Envy didn't take, and they were ready to go.

Envy resembled her mother a lot but she looked identical to her dad. Envy had his dark skinned complexion and good hair similar to someone of Dominican descent that draped just past her shoulders. Envy also took her father's height because at the age of 14, she was about 5'6" tall but only weighed 125 pound. Envy did have her mother's jet black eyebrows and petite shape. Envy was petite but had a nice, apple bottom derrière for her size. Yes, she got a fatty, yal! (LOL)

Mercedes, on the other hand, was a pecan brown complexion and stood only 5'5" tall. Mercedes keeps her hair done by Cherry's Hair Salon on Fulton Street and although she weighed 160 pounds, was just as cute as she was in high school. She was thick but had a nice shape. Mercedes did have a set of Barney's hips like her sisters, Jasmine and Jessica.

Jah looked just like Mercedes, except he was a little darker and much taller, but he and Envy resembled each other as well. Although they resembled one another, Envy was the spitting image of her father Sin who was tall, dark skinned and handsome. Envy had also inherited his pretty skin.

"Meanwhile, back at the ranch…"

It was a few minutes after 11 PM when Mercedes yelled, "ENVY, ARE YOU ABOUT READY?"

"YEA, MA! LET ME COMB MY HAIR DOWN."

“OKAY! CALL A CAB WHEN YOU FINISH. CALL EITHER BLACK PEARL OR UNITED,” Mercedes instructed as she put on her finishing touches.

“OKAY, MA!” Envy yelled back before dialing United Car Service and requesting a cab to pick them up at Gates and Marcus Garvey and drop them off on Myrtle and Nostrand Avenue. “MA, THEY SAID FIVE MINUTES!”

“Okay! Come on, girl. I’m ready.” Mercedes responded.

Envy and her mother left the apartment and when they reached the first floor, the cab was in front of the building. They hopped in and the cab drove down Gates Ave with the windows down while both of them enjoyed the night air and the spring breeze.

Although it was late, the streets were crowded with cars blasting music, girls playing Double Dutch and hopscotch while the boys played a famous street game called Skelly. Every corner store had a crowd in front of it, enjoying the nightlife of Bed-Stuy, one of Brooklyn’s liveliest hoods.

The cab was sitting at a red light on Gates and Marcy when Envy spotted a familiar face.

"Ma, look who is all the way down here," Envy stated as she pointed across the street.

"Crackhead Dawn be everywhere, Envy. Ain't no telling where you will see Dawn at," Mercedes replied.

Dawn was the local hood crackhead. Her stomping ground was the Marcus Garvey end of Bedford Stuyvesant but she got around. Envy was surprised to see her so far away from the neighborhood but kept her eyes on Dawn while the light was red.

"Excuse me, Mister… I like that jersey you got on," Dawn complimented a dude standing on the corner.

"Thanks…"

Before the dude could finish, Dawn interjected, "Do you have a quarter?"

"Nah, I don't have nothing for you, so back the hell up outta my face!" dude snapped and Dawn went off.

"I DON'T KNOW WHO IN THE HELL YOU THINK YOU'RE TALKING TO, BUT YOU BETTA WATCH YOUR MOUTH! I DON'T PLAY

THAT! UTT UNNN," Dawn sarcastically yelled as she twirled her neck and rolled her eyes.

"You dirty crackhead! You betta shut that raggedy pie hole before I slap the spit outta you!"

The light turned green just as Dawn stepped into his face. Envy watched the guy slap Dawn just before the cab turned the corner. The sight of them scuffling with Dawn swinging hysterically before getting tossed to the ground vanished as the cab continued driving. Envy could only wonder about the outcome of the fight.

Envy finally spoke, "Did you see that, Ma? Dawn just mad because dude didn't give her a quarter."

"Yes, that's why I tell you and your brother to stay away from drugs," Mercedes nonchalantly responded.

Dawn always gave a compliment and as soon as you thanked her, you bit the bait. She would then make her move and beg for change. It was something she had done to Envy several times before. She'd always say, "Envy…ooouuu, you are so pretty! I like your hair or shoes," and as soon as Envy thanked her, she would say, "Pretty, do you got a quarter?"

Dawn was known for doing that to everybody. sometimes it worked and sometimes it didn't. And tonight, it looked like it didn't work. Brooklyn was live on a Friday night and Envy knew that once she got to Marcy or Thompkins Projects, things were really going to be poppin'!

Chapter 2

A HARD HEAD MAKE A SOFT BEHIND

Envy was excited when the cab pulled up in the parking lot on the Nostrand Ave side of the PJs only several minutes after she and her mother had gotten in.

"Gimme fi' dolla," the cab driver requested in his Island accent.

Mercedes paid the cab driver, they got out and walked through the projects. The NAGTs were in front of the building rollin' dice and serving feins. The nosey old ladies were sitting on a bench talking about any and everybody that walked by and the chicken heads were cluckin' at whomever. Marcy Projects is a place where the birds be chirping and the baby mommas put their baby daddies on blast in front of everybody. Then there were the bougie chicks, frontin' like they were fab while plotting on their next vic for the night. The bougie chicks would also do nasty things for their change.

Mercedes and Envy spoke to who they knew and disregarded who they didn't know. By the time they reached the building, Envy had a full glimpse of what was what for the night. Basically, Nostrand Ave was poppin' on a Friday night and the weather was nice. Oh, my gosh! There was no telling what was bound to go down in Marcy.

"Woooo, Jesus! This building smells like piss and fish," Mercedes complained as she fanned her hand in front of her face. She then covered her nose and mouth before getting on the elevator.

"Yes, ma, this is disgusting! Why do people pee in the elevator when they are going right inside of an apartment?" Envy asked with her face twisted from the horrible stench.

"People are just nasty and ignorant. There's no telling why people do the things that they do. I guess they have to live up to the fullest potential of the projects," Mercedes tried to explain as the elevator came to a stop on the fourth floor.

"Well, a project is just an experiment. My father once told me that they built projects just to experiment on poor black people. That's why 'they' put guns, drugs, and alcohol in the neighborhood. That's why there is so much violence in or near the projects."

"I see you got something else from your daddy beside his looks," Mercedes stated as they walked down the hallway.

"He told me that they want us to destroy ourselves and our people need to wise up and realize that it's a setup. They fell and still fall for the nonsense, my daddy told me."

Envy went on trying to explain what her dad told her, but Mercedes interrupted while knocking on the door. "I don't know what your father is talking about but if he is so righteous then he needs to be into politics."

Mercedes wasn't too fond of Sin because he left her when Envy was a baby. He stayed in and out of jail, then got married and had a new family. He barely dealt with Envy during her younger years when she needed him most. So Mercedes' feelings were personal because she was left to raise Envy and Jah on her own.

Jah's biological father had passed away when Jah was 1 year old, so that was hard on her as well. The sad part was that Sin lived nearby on the Park Ave side of Marcy Projects with his wife and was making more children while barely acknowledging Envy's presence. All Mercedes wanted was for him to help raise his daughter and teach her what and what not to accept from a man. It would've been nice had he shown Envy certain things that Mercedes couldn't. But instead, Sin chose the streets and the wife that was fit for his lifestyle.

"Meanwhile, back at the ranch…"

Someone finally opened the door to where the card game was being held. They walked into the apartment and greeted everyone. A seat was immediately available for Mercedes while Envy made her way to the back of the apartment to inform her cousins Nay and Taya of what and who she'd just seen outside.

"Yo, Bliilzes (Bliilzes was a name that Nay and Envy would call each other), I just saw Ant, Shawn, Raquel and all of them rollin' dice. Oh my God! Ant just looks sooo good, son," Envy boasted when she entered Nay's bedroom.

"Taya, you hungry?" Nay asked while Envy gloated.

"Yea, why? Taya answered.

"Because we should ask Mommy for some money to get some Chinese food so that we can go downstairs. I wanna see Rah," Nay responded, making it clear that she wanted to see one of Ant's younger brothers.

The girls did as they had plotted.

"Hey, Ma, me and Taya are real hungry. Can we get some Chinese food?" Nay humbly asked.

"Yal know not to come ask me for anything while I'm playing cards. Now take this $10 and get the hell out of my face!" Stacey shouted.

"Ma, can I go with them?" Envy asked Mercedes, whose focus was on the card game.

"Envy, you shouldn't be hungry because we just ate before we got here," Mercedes responded.

"I'm not hungry, Ma. I just wanna walk with them so that I won't be here by myself," Envy responded.

"Go head, and you better come right back," Mercedes demanded without looking at Envy.

The girls immediately began too prissy up. Envy was the first one in the mirror while Nay and Taya were putting their shoes and stuff on.

"Envy, move over. I need to fix my hair," Nay demanded as she bumped Envy to move over.

"Wait! I'm not done yet," Envy replied, trying to push her way back in front of the mirror.

"Ain't nothing wrong with you, Envy. You know that you just left out of the mirror before you left home," Taya jumped in.

"It's time for me to go back to Nancy's to get a fresh wash and set. This one is wearing off," Envy replied as she and Nay shared the mirror.

"We just went last week. We have a whole week before we need to go back," Nay responded, knowing that their parents had them on a two-week schedule to get their hair washed and set.

"Well, maybe I need a perm because mine won't lay right and I just bumped it," Envy stated as she finished her last touches. Both she and Nay were ready to go.

"C'mon, Taya. You ready?" Nay asked.

"Yea, I'm ready. Let me pee first."

Envy and Nay burst out laughing and picking with Taya, saying that she was nervous because Quan was outside. These girls were typical teenagers and had such serious crushes on these guys that they were so scared to walk past them but love to peep at them.

Whenever they walked past the group of boys, they would get all silly and ask each other, “Is he looking at me? Is he looking over here? Oh, my gosh! What is he doing now?”

They would go through all of that instead of just walking up to the guys and speaking to them. Ladies, you know exactly what I’m talking about! Don’t front! LOL

That was always Envy’s problem. She was shy and afraid of rejection. Even though Envy was a pretty dark skinned girl with gorgeous skin and baby doll features, she still wasn’t satisfied with her complexion. Growing up, she was always teased by her mother and Jah, and anyone that she argued with had something to say about her skin color. She resented the harsh names they called her, like blacky, black tar baby, black spasm and a few others not worth mentioning.

Once Taya was done, the girls went on their mission, literally. By the time they reached the first floor, the guys had made it inside of the building to gamble. The police must’ve run them from outside, as usual.

“Damn, Envy! Your backyard is bangin’ like it’s busy,” Ant stated as Envy walked past him and all Envy did was smile. “Com’ere, Envy, let me holla at you for a minute.”

Envy continued smiling as she walked over to Ant who was biting gently on his bottom lip. His navy blue New York Yankees baseball cap was pulled down to his eyebrows as he waited patiently for Envy to get in front of him.

"What's up with you? I wanted to holla at you earlier but you were with Moms and you know I'm not testing Miss Cedes," Ant stated.

"Yea, that was the best thing to do because I would never hear the end of it. But I'm chilln', about to go to the Chinese restaurant," Envy spoke softly.

Ant's eyes were moving up and down Envy's body when he flirtatiously said, "Damn, you lookin' good, Ma! Yal going to that party in Tompkins PJs?"

"Thank you, and yea, we are about to go to Tompkins after we leave the Chinese restaurant," Envy responded.

"C'mon, son. You holdin' up the game. Don't get scared now because you know that I'm about to take your money!" Quan hollered at Ant.

Ant laughed then stated, "Aiight, Envy, Ima catch up with you at the party. Make sure you save me a dance."

"Aiight," Envy stated as she walked away, noticing that Nay was still conversing with Raquel. When Nay was done, the girls walked to Marcy Ave to the Chinese restaurant and ordered their food. Once they got the food, they decided to sit, eat and talk about the boys.

"Envy, you be starvin' for Ant. You was chees'n' mad hard when he called your name," Nay stated and she and Taya started laughing.

"Mind your business because ain't nobody say anything about how you were looking dead in Raquel's eyes when he was talking to you," Envy snapped back.

"Oh, wait a minute you didn't see Taya talking to Quan? She was looking down at her feet the whole time. She was the one that was really scared and nervous," Nay stated as she and Envy laughed.

"Mind your ugly business, Nay! You always gotta put me in it," Taya responded.

"Don't get mad, baldy, because you thought that nobody ain't see you," Nay quickly returned fire.

"But anyway, I can't wait to get to this party," Envy said on purpose just to interrupt the argument that was on its way.

Nay and Taya always argued.

"Me neither," Nay responded to Envy's comment.

"I'm not going because we are gonna get in trouble. We didn't ask can we go to Tompkins," Taya stated with concern.

"Oh boy, Taya. There you go acting like a square!" Envy teased.

"By the time they realize that we are gone, we will be back. You know that once they get into them cards, they are stuck till the sun comes up. We're good," Nay responded. "Stop being a punk, Taya.

Somehow, someway, they talked Taya into going with them to the party. Once they arrived in Tompkins, the party was poppin'! It was at this dude named Man Man's crib. They played the hottest reggae, Biggie, Jay, and Nas.

Aerie, who was the local DJ, started remixin' some B.I.G and the crowd went bananas as the lyrics to "Where's Brooklyn at?" played repeatedly.

All of the windows were wide open as everyone continued to dance and sweat like there was no tomorrow and when Method Man's anthem (M.E.T.H.O.D M.A.N) came on, everyone was singing in sync.

It was an official Brooklyn party and Envy and her cousins were having a ball. And just when you thought the party couldn't get any better, the DJ threw on "Hard Knock Life" by Jay-Z and everybody really reps for Jay. C'mon! It was a Marcy and Tompkins party, which is Jay's home, so the crowd went bananas!

Envy and Taya were dancing together when they spotted Ant and the crew coming through the door. The girls were so sweated out from the crowd and the excitement that they didn't even want to face the guys but just as they walked up, the DJ went back to playing some reggae music and Ant grabbed Envy, Raquel grabbed Nay and Quan grabbed Taya and it was on. The girls gave the guys the "dub" (dub is whining on a dude mad hard to the rhythm and beat of a song especially reggae) of their life.

Then Little Vicious' song "Freaks" followed and it was on. OH MY GOSH! That was the HIT!!! That's when Envy noticed that she and her cousins were the envy of the party. They had the attention of the poppin' older dudes. All eyes were on them so they showed off even more. After about five songs, the girls finally decided that the boys were hard enough so they let up off of their penises for a while. You ladies know what I'm talking about.

At about 2:30 in the morning, Aerie announced that the party was over before he ran the famous line, "YAL AIN'T GOTTA GO HOME BUT YAL GOTTA GET THE HELL UP OUTTA HERE! AND SOME OF YAL NEED TO WASH BEFORE COMING TO A PARTY, ALL I SMELL IS FISH AND FEET!!" And he was never lying.

The music had stopped, the lights came on and everyone was making their way out of the hot apartment. Although the party was over, the real action was about to begin. Most of the people in the party had taken the stairs but Envy and her cousins decided to wait for the elevator. When the elevator door opened, there was a group of girls already on the elevator. Something told Envy not to get on the elevator but she didn't follow her gut. -Wrong move!

They got on the elevator anyway and the females burst out in laughter. What Envy and 'em didn't know was that the girls were plotting to jump them from the moment they started going hard in the party.

Real Brooklyn chicks know that dirty bum chicks love to disgrace anything that's clean. So after the elevator started moving, the lights went out. It was total chaos as someone pulled on Envy's hair and someone slapped the hell out of Taya. Nay was fighting with a girl that had jumped on her from behind. The girls fought back as much and hard as they could even though they were outnumbered. They were throwing down and they refused to hit the ground. It was an all-out brawl and everyone was throwing blows at everyone, STRAIGHT UP!

When the elevator door opened, Ant and his crew, who had been waiting for Envy and her cousins, broke up the fight.

"GET THE HELL OUTTA HERE AND GET OFF OF 'EM! YAL BUM BROADS STAY JUMPING SOMEBODY!" Ant yelled as he grabbed Envy and 'em, who still wanted to fight.

"YAL RAGGEDY BUMS AIN'T ABOUT THIS LIFE!" Nay yelled as Raquel held her back.

"YAL CAN'T EVEN FIGHT, LIKE 10 OF YAL JUMPED US AND I DON'T SEE BLOOD OR BLACK EYES NOWHERE! I WILL FIGHT ALL OF YAL ONE ON ONE! WHAT'S POPPIN'?!" Envy yelled out of anger, but she was dead serious.

Envy was a fighter. She may have been young but her hands were lethal. She didn't get into many fights but the ones that she had, Envy had won them all. Her cousin Taya was scrappy with the hands as well and she had never lost a fight even though she was the quiet one. Now Nay, on the other hand, wasn't really a fighter but she would fight if she had to. Envy and Taya always protected Nay because she was only 4'11 and skinny. Envy and Taya were on the slim side too but they both had height on them.

"Meanwhile, back at the ranch…"

As Envy ran up to hit one of the girls, Ant grabbed her. "Nah, Envy. It ain't worth it. All they wanna do is jump yal. You too pretty for this, Ma!"

"SO WHAT, ANT! THEY MESSED UP MY HAIR! LET US FIGHT! THEY CAUGHT US OFF GUARD BUT NOW WE'RE READY," Nay yelled, still trying to get away from Raquel.

"COME ON, WADDUP? ONE ON ONE… YAL MAD BECAUSE YAL GOT STOMPED!" this big dark skinned girl with a scar on her face and no hair shouted out.

"STOMPED WHO!? Yal can't fight! All you do is pull hair! Get your hands up before yal try to step to us! That's why yal had to jump us!" Taya shot back with malice in her voice.

Ant and his crew were able to get Envy and 'em out the building and into his homeboy Adam's car. Adam drove the girls back to Nostrand Ave while Ant and the crew walked. The girls were finally quiet because as they pulled up to Marcy Projects, immediately noticed Mercedes, and she was not alone. She was with Stacey, Laura, Carrie, Neila and Michelle. It was the entire card crew and they were headed toward Tompkins.

In the hood, news spread quickly. Laura, Carrie, Neila, and Michelle were Stacey's sisters and when one rolled, they all rolled.

"WHO IN THE HELL TOLD YAL TO TAKE YAL GROWN BEHINDS TO A GOT DAMN PARTY?" Stacey screamed as Envy and her cousins exited the car.

"AND ENVY, YOU KNOW BETTER! You wanna get over here and show off, huh? Yal better say goodbye because it will be a long time before yal see Envy again," Mercedes stated, disappointed in her daughter.

"FORGET ALL OF THAT... WHO WAS YOU FIGHTING?" Laura questioned as the stench of liquor on her breath.

Laura was Stacey's youngest sister. She and Carrie were no joke, especially Carrie, so they were ready to get it in. They would worry about Envy and 'em being sneaky later.

"Come on, Laura. We're going over there. Stacey, yal can go ahead and leave. We got this," Carrie stated as she and Laura walked away. Stacey, Mercedes and their girls walked to the corner of Myrtle and Nostrand and caught a cab and went home. Once they were in the cab, Mercedes let Envy have it.

"Envy, you are getting out of control! Now do you see why I don't let you go anywhere by yourself?"

"But Ma, they started," Envy cried in defense.

"Shut up while I'm talking. You said enough when you lied and asked if you can go to the Chinese restaurant! Don't say another word to me. You are on punishment for a long time, little girl. Something worse could've happened to yal out there at 2:30 in the morning and we would have never known. Yal hot behinds were at a party!? I see you're going to make me hurt you. At some damn party this time of the morning," Mercedes continued fussing as Envy just frowned while staring out the window.

The cab finally reached Gates Ave. and oh boy, was Envy glad to get out of that car because Mercedes had been fussing since the time they got in.

She'd just gotten jumped and hearing her mother scolding her was the last thing that she wanted to hear, regardless if she was wrong or right, so she decided to tune her out.

When they reached the apartment, Mercedes got even more furious to find that Jah wasn't home.

"Now I told this boy to be home by 11:30 and he ain't here! Oh Lord, what am I going to do with these kids? Please, God, give me strength!"

Envy went straight to bed but could hear Mercedes still cursing and fussing at no one. The last thing Envy heard her mother say was, "A hard head make a soft behind."

Chapter 3

DEATH HITS CLOSE TO HOME

It was Saturday afternoon when Jah finally returned home. Thank God Mercedes had choir rehearsal, therefore she wasn't home when Jah got there. Envy was usually able to go to her Aunt Jasmine's house to chill with her cousin Chelsea who was also like a little sister whenever Mercedes went to rehearsal. Being that Envy was on punishment for what happened the night before, she had to stay in the house.

"Ooouuuuuu, Jah, you in trrrrouble… Mommy is mad at you," Envy picked at her brother.

"For real, Envy? What did she say?"

"She said that we are too grown, we don't listen and we will be 18 before we see outside again other than school and church," Envy exaggerated just a little.

"You in trouble, too?" Jah cautiously asked.

“Yea, I went to a party in Tompkins last night and got into a fight. These girls jumped me, Nay, and Taya.”

“But mommy don’t even know what happened to me so she can’t be mad at me. But what were you doing at a party in Tompkins?” Jah inquired.

Envy quickly lied, “When I asked Mommy if I can go, she nodded her head yea, but she was playing cards, so she doesn't remember doing that. Those Sumner Project girls were hating on us. We got on the elevator and one of them busted out the lights, next thing you know, we felt punches!” Envy started before laughing. “So we went for what we knew. Somebody told Mommy and ‘em, and by the time they were on the way over there, we were back.” Envy made sure not to mention Ant’s name because Jah knew that she had a crush on him.

“You gotta show me who these dirty chicks are because I do fight girls and since they want to jump people, watch what I do. They all be sweating me anyway!” Jah was upset because he hated for anyone to touch Envy. He even got mad if their mom hit her, that’s how over protective he was with his little sister. So he was on a mission to find the girls.

About an hour later, Mercedes came home. Jah had the nerve to have his best friend Corey in the house, knowing that he was in trouble. He thought maybe Corey's presence could save him. Even though he was nervous, he greeted his Mom, "Hey, Ma, how was church?"

"Hey, Ma, nothing! You know that you are in big trouble. Where were you last night? I told you to be in this house by 11:30. I came home at 3 am and you still weren't here! Yal kids are getting beside yal self. When you get too grown to listen to me then you don't need to be here!"

Mercedes went on before she finally noticed Corey sitting on the couch. Corey was scared to speak because she'd caught him laughing.

"How you you you doing, Ms. Cedes?" he stuttered.

"Hi, Corey, but you can go home because Jah ain't going nowhere and can't have no company for a long time."

Corey did as he was told and went home. After Corey left, Jah folded. "But Ma, I'm sorry for staying out. I was at the hospital all night. Ty got killed last night," Jah explained before bursting into tears.

"Oh my God, I'm sorry to hear that baby but you still could've called or something. See there, one of your friends got killed. It could've been you, and I wouldn't have known a thing. That's what I'm talking about. I worry when you do things like that. Now, what happened to Ty?" Mercedes asked after using the moment to confirm how dangerous the streets could be.

"We were sitting on the bench at 44 Park around one in the morning and some dudes just rolled up on us in a black car with the windows tinted. No one noticed it when it came to a complete stop and the back window slowly rolled down. Ty screamed for everybody to run and pulled out his gun but it was too late. They got to shooting at us and we all scattered. Ty's gun got jammed and when the shots finally stopped, he was lying face down on the side of the bench. So me, Corey, and Shane ran back toward Ty just as he took his last breath. The dudes drove off and all we saw was blood coming out of Ty's mouth," Jah explained the glory details as he cried like a baby and Mercedes wrapped her arms around him.

"I feel so sorry for his mother. I don't know what I would do if it was you. Jah, how old was Ty?" Mercedes asked after she placed her arm around his shoulder.

Jah was wiping his face with his brand new Polo shirt when he responded in between sniffles, "He was 16."

"Jah, you need to get some rest. I know this is pretty rough for you. But do you see why I say that a hard head makes a soft behind? You ask can you go to St Marks and I told to be home by 11: 30 and you didn't listen. Not only were you not where you asked to be but look at the time that you were out there. I keep telling y'all kids that there's nothing out after midnight but trouble. For all of your disobedience, you witnessed one of your best friends get killed. I feel for you. I love you and me and Envy will help you get through this," Mercedes stated as she kissed Jah's forehead and encouraged him to take a shower and get some rest.

That was the beginning of the end of Jah's pain. He then realized that the streets are cold. Kill or be killed was the heart that it gave him. Jah, Ty, Corey, and Shane were all best friends. They'd started their little Blood clique 9-Trey gangstas with just the four of them and one of Ty's little cousins was being recruited. For years it was just the four of them and they all got along like brothers. So yes, this tragedy was really hard on Jah.

After he took a shower, he stayed in bed all night crying and blaming his friend's death on himself.

*   *   *   *   *

(Junior High School 324)

Monday morning, as usual, India, one of Envy's best friends, was ringing her bell for school. And as usual, Envy was not ready, therefore India had to wait an extra 30 minutes for her. Envy finally came downstairs.

"Damn, Envy, what takes you so long? You be getting me in trouble because the school tells my mother that I'm late every day and she scream at me because she knows that I leave the house at 7:15."

"My bad, India, but my mother always gotta fuss and want somebody to do something for her," Envy spat out a lie really fast to avoid the shame of the truth.

What had happened was Envy was 14 and still peeing in the bed! This particular morning, she'd peed in her mother's bed and her mother woke her up at 6:30 to go to the laundry. So by the time India got to Envy's house, Envy was just getting dressed. Envy quickly changed the subject after promising India that it wouldn't happen again.

"India, did you hear about Ty getting killed Friday night?"

"Ty from where?" India quickly asked as they walked to school.

"Ty from Gates and Throop (Troop is how they pronounce it), my brother's friend," Envy explained.

"OH MY GOODNESS! ENVY, STOP LYING!!!!" India shouted with her sensitive self. India would cry over anything. Envy always called her a punk.

"Yes, India. Somebody shot him in the chest over there by 44 Park."

"I heard that somebody got shot but I didn't know that it was Ty. I tried to call you a couple of times but Auntie said that you were on punishment," India responded, addressing Mercedes as Auntie. Envy and India were close like sisters. India burst into tears after learning that it was Ty who had gotten murdered over the weekend.

"Shut up, India, and wipe your face before we go to this store," Envy demanded while displaying no empathy for her friend's feelings.

India begins wiping her face and trying her best to dry her eyes. The store on the corner of Gates and Stuyvesant was crowded every morning and every afternoon. The line was packed because half the school was ordering a bagel with cream cheese and jelly. That was the bomb!! Envy would buy 5 packs of gum and India usually joined the crowd that was buying bagels. But this particular morning, the store was waaaaay too crowded and the girls were extremely late for school.

As usual, Envy convinced India to walk through the yellow side, which was the entrance for Special Ed, where Envy's junior high sweetheart David was being educated.

Once inside the school, they ran into him and Envy and David went through their morning routine. David would wrestle with Envy and take at least 3 of her 5 packs of gum. She knew they were love taps, nothing serious.

Once the girls got to class, they were greeted by their teacher, Mr. Givens, and classmates.

"WHAT UP, ENVY? WHAT YOU DOING WITH THAT TRICK?" Izel, a troublemaker in their class, shouted.

“Miss Izel, watch your mouth before I send you to Dean Barrett or Ms. Metz,” Mr. Givens threatened.

“Oh, my bad, Mr. Givens,” Izel apologized with a smirk on her face.

“Izel, stop starting,” Envy requested as she sat across from Izel and Cheyenne.

“Nah, Envy. You know I don’t like ‘Essay’,” Izel stated as she burst out into laughter knowing that India heard her.

People would call India “Essay” because they said that she looked like the Arabs in the corner stores and the Arabs called everybody “Essay.”

“I know, Izel, but leave her alone,” Envy said, defending her friend as she blushed, knowing why Izel was starting with India.

Izel didn’t like Envy’s relationship with India, so she was always teasing India. India was not a fighter, but she would talk some junk! She was too pretty to fight, though. People would actually hit her and she wouldn’t do anything about it. That’s how Envy and India became besties. Envy used to pick on India as well before they became best friends.

The first day of school, the class was assigned a group project. Envy was not interested in doing her class project at all. But India approached her and said, "Envy, we live in the next building from each other, maybe we can partner up and do our project together?"

"Yeah, sure! It sounds good to me," Envy nonchalantly replied.

The girls did as they'd planned. They teamed up at the library after school almost every day for two weeks until the project was completed. The time they spent with one another forced them to bond and when the project was done, India wanted to be friends with Envy. Envy agreed, and they became besties from then on.

Now Izel and Envy became besties because the both of them were beasts. Izel was only 4'11" and skinny but a feisty little girl. She was no threat to Envy. She and Envy clicked automatically after hearing about each other's reputations and had been besties from then on as well. However, Izel and India never really got along.

"So what's good with you, Cheyenne?" Envy asked after dismissing Izel's antics.

"Nothing much. My Aunt Sheila is not home so we were just talking about a hooky party being that it's the first day of summer," Cheyenne responded.

"Oh, word... That sounds good to me. What time are we leaving? And who's going to be there?" Envy asked with excitement in her tone.

"We are trying to leave after the second period, and I'm inviting everybody. I'm not sure who all will show up but ShaGary is bringing the music. He and I discussed it last night, and I told him to bring his latest CDs," Cheyenne continued explaining as they ignored Mr. Givens.

"Did you invite David and 'em?" Envy curiously asked, of course.

"Nah… I didn't get a chance to invite them yet but I will, or maybe you can tell him after class. Who else should I invite because you and Izel really don't like females?" Cheyenne stated.

"Invite Enrique and his brothers, and Kebo and 'em…"

As Envy continued with names, Izel interrupted, "UGH! Listen to this chick naming all of the light skinned dudes!!!" They all burst out laughing.

"First of all, Izel, you need to mind your business!" Envy boldly snap back with a Kool-Aid smile on her face.

"Naaah, Boo-Boo! Don't get mad at me because you got jungle fever," Izel responded.

"Anyway, let me see if India wants to come. I'm not listening to you Izel."

As Envy walked toward India's seat, she was hit in the back of her head with a paper ball. Everyone who saw it burst out laughing.

Envy quickly turned around and said, "Stop playing with me!" Envy noticed BoBo with a big Kool-Aid smile. "I know that it was you, BoBo. Stop playing with me," she repeated as she rolled her eyes in a flirtatious way and continued over toward India.

Envy and BoBo had a secret crush on each other. Envy approached India and whispered, "India, Cheyenne's Aunt Sheila is not home. It's a hooky party going down at her crib. Do you want to come?"

"Who's going?" India whispered back, knowing her answer might be no because of Izel.

"Well, for now, it's me, Izel, Cheyenne, and ShaGary."

"Nah, Envy. Ima chill just in case Auntie come so I can cover for you. You know how she does, pop up out of nowhere. But really, you need to stay your butt in school. That's why you're failing now, because you have been cutting too much lately. Every time you get with your little friends, you cut class!" India sarcastically stated.

"First of all, India, you swear that you know everything. You need to mind your business," Envy began to bash India for looking out for her.

Class finally ended. Envy, Izel, and Cheyenne were trying to gather the crowd for the party.

"Hold up, yal. Let me get some water. Izel, walk me to the water fountain," Envy asked and Izel followed her.

As Envy leaned forward to sip the water, this rude ghetto chick came over. A chick named Vikki jumped in front of Envy on purpose and busted out laughing as she sipped the water while glancing back at Envy.

"Yo, this chick is playing herself! I can't stand her boney, UGH!" Envy stated as she shook her head in disgust.

Vikki walked away laughing and shaking water off of her hands. She was trying to be a bully, but what she didn't know was she was barking up the wrong tree. Vikki and her crew were the so-called bad girls of the school all because they were from Brevoort Projects, which were on the other side of Bedford-Stuyvesant. But to Envy and Izel, they weren't about that life!

"I should go snatch that cheap weave out of her head," Envy angrily spoke out loud while staring at Vikki as she walked away.

"Yo, Envy, damn that bird! We'll catch her later. Let's go have some fun."

"You right. But I owe that chick one," Envy responded before they continued gathering people for the hooky party of the year.

And at that moment, Vikki marked herself as an enemy to Envy. Vikki had no idea that Envy was that Brooklyn chick but it was something she would shortly find out.

Chapter 4

THE HOOKY PARTY

It was going down directly after the first period class ended. A group of kids had gathered at separate locations to sneak out of school for a hooky party at Cheyenne's house. They plotted for some of them to sneak out of the doors on the Monroe side and some of them would sneak out on the Gates Avenue side. The news had spread quickly and those that couldn't get out one of the two exits planned to meet at Cheyenne's house.

Although the party was supposed to start at 9:30, it didn't get popping until almost 11. Everyone was having a good time and the music was live thanks to ShaGary. Everything was going well until the wild pack came through.

David was the first one to enter and his brother Kah was right behind him as usual. They had BoBo, Spliff, and the whole Malcolm X Boulevard crew and everyone had a brown bag with some liquor inside of it. They were smoking, dancing, and running all through the house. They started a game of corners, boys against girls. There was a group in Cheyenne's room playing spin the bottle while a strip poker game was going down in the dining room. Around 12 o'clock, someone turned off all the lights and things got a little out of control.

Cheyenne ended the party at 2:30 and the house was a wreck. Envy and Izel stayed later to help her clean but the crib was a mess. Things were broken, the carpet was stained with alcohol and there were holes burnt on the sofa and ashes on the coffee table. The crib was also smoked out although they had opened every window in the house. Cheyenne was in big trouble.

Envy and Izel left Cheyenne crying and trying to figure out what she was going to tell her aunt. The two of them decided to walk by the school to scope the scene. They were exchanging stories about the hooky party when they spotted someone they knew. It was Envy's lucky day because guess who was walking down the street? VIKKI!

"Ooooo, baby! Izel, look who I see," Envy spoke in a devilish voice. "And she's by herself. I'm about to press her. I got to so she won't ever violate me again like she did earlier. She got to feel me like she needs to," Envy concluded with her eyes locked on Vikki.

"I got you, girl," Izel responded as both girls waited for traffic to ease up in order to cross the street to where Vikki was.

Vikki's back was facing them as Envy and Izel crossed the street and crept up behind her. "Aye, Vikki, come here for a minute. Let me holla at you," Envy spoke loudly as they got closer.

Vikki turned around, stopped and looked around before responding, "Who, me?" She had a confused look on her face, unlike the smirk she'd had in school earlier.

"Yes, you. You are the only one over there," Envy spat back as they stepped to her.

"Hold up, little gir…"

Before she could finish, Envy interrupted, "Is there a problem? Do we have an issue or something?"

"First of all, I don't even know you," Vikki lied.

"Yea, that's what I thought, but the way that you jumped in front of me at the water fountain earlier, I assumed we had some type of issue that needed to be solved!" Envy said as she stepped directly into Vikki's face. "Forget all of the small talk since you're playing dumb! I'm letting you know now, if you EVER try to play me again, we will most definitely have a problem," Envy spoke while pointing in her face, trying to entice a fight.

"But I don't remember doing that to you. I don't know what you're talking about," Vikki tried to explain.

"Envy, let's bounce. We already knew that she's a school bully. She ain't about that life we live. She knows exactly what you're talking about. She knows what you're saying and as long as she doesn't try to play you again, we're good," Izel stated and Envy nodded, agreeing with her. Envy sucked her teeth and they turned to walk away when Vikki had something else to say.

"Let me go get Dreia," Vikki spoke, sounding a little cocky.

"Nah, ma. You don't gotta go get nobody. We can do it all right here, RIGHT NOW!" Envy quickly responded with an attitude.

SMACK!

Envy then slapped the hell out of Vikki and she took a step back after grabbing the left side of her face. Izel and Envy moved in closer simultaneously as Vikki began jogging away.

"Okay, you got it! It ain't nothing!" Vikki said after slipping between two parked cars.

The girls walked away laughing hard.

"Envy, you are a bully!" Izel joked.

"No, I'm not. Everyone saw what she did earlier. Bet if her crew was around just now, she would've tried to pop slick. Watch tomorrow she try to play like she that chick. And I'm going to stomp her out in front of her crew. She gets no more chances!" Envy said, frustrated that Vikki backed down so easily.

"I'm surprised that you let her rock with that one. The Envy I know would've rocked her when she pulled that little water fountain stunt."

"The only reason I let her rock for one, is because we were trying to do us and get out and dodge before we got noticed, and two, I don't need any reason for my mother to come up to the school questioning them about a fight for her to find out that I cut school. That would be double trouble for me. I'm already on punishment for going to Man-Man's party in Tompkins Friday night."

"Oh my gosh! Envy, you went?" Izel excitedly responded.

“Yes, and why did me and my cousins Nay and Taya get jumped by some chicks from your hood?”

“Envy, you’re lying. Damn, I wish that I was there but my mother was drunk and trippin’. So I snuck and chilled with Ritty before he got drunk and passed out. And I started to tell him to walk over there with me, too. Damn, girl!”

“He was in the party. I saw him with Mike and Ant and ’em,” Envy replied.

“Oh, word, son!! That dude be lying too much for me. But here comes my bus. Ima call you later,” Izel stated as she walked away to meet the bus.

Izel jumped on the B 15 and Envy continued to walk down Gates toward her house. She only had one more block to go, and Marcus Garvey was the next corner. By the time Envy reached her building, 685 Gates Avenue, it was chaos. All of these girls were screaming and hollering. Dudes were consoling them, and everybody was huddled up like something was seriously wrong

“What up, Envy? You heard what happened to Ty from down the block?” Kara asked Envy when she walked up on her.

"Yeah, son, that was crazy! Oh, that's why everybody's over there?"

"Yea, his little brother Tre is going crazy. I feel so sorry for him," Kara added while shaking her head.

"I thought that was his little cousin, but damn, it is sad," Envy sympathized.

"I wanna know what really happened," Kara stated.

"Well then ride with me upstairs. I'll tell you because my brother was there."

Kara and Envy rode the elevator and Kara was quiet while Envy gave her all of the details that Jah had given her and her mom. After getting off of the elevator, Envy went her way and Kara went her way. Kara's apartment was around the hallway corner from Envy's and they were pretty close as well.

Kara was the first person that Envy met when she moved into the building at age 6. Envy and Kara both went to P.S 44, so they labeled themselves as cousins, and then found out that their family members shared the same mutual friends which drew them even closer. After elementary school, Kara went to Choir Academy and Envy went to 324, so they grew a little distant but never apart.

"Hi, Ma. How are you doing today?" Envy asked as she hugged her mother after entering the apartment. Envy tried to be as nice as possible, checking her mother's spirit to see if she was aware of her ditching school.

Basically, Envy was guilty and, as usual, Mercedes would allow her and Jah to get their rocks off by letting them think that it was nothing, and as soon as they thought it was over, she would drop the bomb.

Envy walked into the room only to see Jah lying in bed. "Hey, Jah, are you okay?"

"Yea, Envy. I'm aiight," he responded in a soft tone, voice still cracking as if he'd been crying.

Envy knew her brother very well because they were around each other 24/7. They were never apart unless they were outside with their friends, so Envy knew that Jah wasn't alright. He had been in bed all weekend and it made Envy cry to see and hear her brother in that state. Tears immediately began to stream down Envy's face before she could catch herself. Envy went into the bathroom and did a little sneaky cry and came back out like nothing never happened.

“Envy, come here. Dora wants to speak to you and make it quick because you know that you can’t have no phone calls,” Mercedes stated as she handed Envy the phone.

“What’s up, Dora?” Envy said.

“ENVY, WHY YOU AIN’T TELL ME THAT MY BOO GOT KILLED!?” Dora yelled into the phone with her loud self.

“Aww, man, I’m on punishment and couldn’t use the phone,” Envy answered.

“OH, WELL, YOU COULD’VE FOUND A WAY TO TELL ME! I BET INDIA AND ‘EM KNOW WHAT HAPPENED! BET YOU FOUND A WAY TO TELL THEM!” Dora yelled again.

Dora got on everybody’s nerves because her mouth was so big and her attitude was so stank, but Envy loved her to death. Dora and Chelsea were like Envy’s sisters and no one ever came between that but you couldn’t tell Dora that. She would always start a big thing with Envy by saying that she loved her friends more than she loved her.

“Whatever, Dora. Anyway, I gotta go. I’ll call you back and let you know all of the details when I can.”

The girls hung up the phone.

Just as Envy was about to walk out of her mother's room, Mercedes dropped the bomb. "So Envy, why did you leave school early today?"

Envy turned and stuttered, "Uh, uh, huh, Ma?" That's when she made herself hot. Mercedes knew everything else from there was a lie.

"I said why did you leave school today? And don't make me have to ask you again," Mercedes spoke firmly and a very calm tone.

"I didn't leave school. Who told you that?" Envy asked with the dumb face.

"Ms. Metz called, but since she's lying on you, then maybe I need to call her right now so that we can get this straight," Mercedes said while preparing to call Ms. Metz.

"No, Ma. You don't have to call her. I only went to the store to get some cough drops because I wasn't feeling good and I didn't wanna keep coughing in class," Envy came up with a quick, bold faced lie.

"Oh! So a bunch of yal didn't run straight out the doors? As a matter of fact, don't answer. I have to go up there tomorrow anyway, so we will just see exactly what happened. Until then, go to your room and stay there until I call you out."

Envy was scared to death of the thought that her mother had to go up to her school. She couldn't understand why she was so unlucky. It seemed like she kept getting caught with everything that she had been doing lately. To ease her mind, Envy went and played her Super Nintendo. *Super Mario World* was her favorite. She loved for Mario to get the wings and fly with Yoshi. She played the game until she got tired and fell asleep.

The next day, Mercedes went up to the school and found out the truth. Envy's punishment was extended, not to mention that she got suspended from school for a week.

The week went by slowly and Envy cried every day that she saw her brother hurt. Jah stayed in the house and in the bed all week. She couldn't focus on her own issues because she was catering to Jah, who barely ate or talked to anyone.

Ty's wake was Thursday evening and the funeral was Friday morning. Jah tried to cover his pain in front of everybody. But he, Corey and Shane expressed their pain to one another. It was the kind of pain that lasts a lifetime.

As far as Envy, the walls and the Mario Brothers had become her new life until she could find a reason to hit the streets once again.

Chapter 5

BACK TO SCHOOL WITH A NEW ATTITUDE

Envy was surprised Monday morning to find that her mother had bought her a brand new pair of Reeboks. 54/11s were what they called them because that was exactly how much they cost, tax included. She already had every color. Reeboks and Air Max 95s were her favorites. The white patent leather Reeboks with the ridges on the bottom had just come out Saturday.

When Mercedes saw them on Graham Avenue while passing Tom, Dick and Harry's, which was the hood's hottest sneaker store, Mercedes knew that Envy would love them, not to mention that it was Envy's last day of punishment.

Envy had to find the best outfit to go with the sneakers. She finally decided on her black and white pleated skirt on top of her white tights. She then found some matching black and white socks go with it. She figured a white turtleneck would do the job, and she knew just where to find one.

Envy called India at 7 A.M. and when India heard her voice, she assumed that something was definitely up. India answered the phone in a puzzled tone, "What's up, Envy? What are you doing calling me this early?"

"Shut up. You act like I don't be up this early," Envy quickly responded.

"No, you don't!" India spat back.

"Okay, whatever! But I'm calling to see if you have a white turtleneck? My mother brought me the new Reeboks…"

"Let me guess. The white patent leather with the ridges on the bottom?" India interrupted before Envy could finish.

"Yes, how do you know?"

"Because I got the same ones yesterday and I can't figure out what to wear with them," India explained.

"Well, I'm trying to wear my black and white pleated skirt with my white tights and matching socks. I was thinking about wearing a white turtleneck with it because my black one doesn't look right," Envy continued.

"Oh, I could wear mine, too, and since I have black tights, I could lend you my white turtleneck and wear your black one," India stated.

"Okay, that sounds good! I'll see you when you get here."

The girls ended their phone call and continued to get dressed.

By 7:25 A.M., India was there to pick Envy up. They switched shirts and left for school. You couldn't tell them that they weren't fly that day. As they walked down Gates Avenue, one of their haters, a grown lady named Blacky, yelled out of her window, "LOOK AT THE BOPSEY TWINS LOOKING LIKE STUPID TRAMPS!" She then started laughing as loud as she could.

Both the girls looked up at her and Envy's face was twisted as if she was about to say something when India spoke first, "Envy, don't even pay her no attention because I know you're about to say something."

But, to India's surprise, all Envy did was turn around and stick her middle finger up. "I can kill her easy just by flicking her off. Look at her old and miserable self just sitting in the window at 7:30 in the morning starting with us. She's a bum and she gets no attention," Envy said and they both just burst out laughing.

"I KNOW YAL LITTLE GIRLS AIN'T SAY NOTHING SLICK BECAUSE I WILL COME DOWNSTAIRS AND BEAT THE MESS OUT OF BOTH OF YAL!" Blacky yelled from her second-floor apartment window.

"COME DO IT, AIN'T NOBODY RUNNING!" Envy finally yelled back, unable to hold it in anymore.

"Oh, my goodness! Envy, don't pay her no mind. We have to get to school, not to mention she is a lonely old lady."

"India, be quiet. Ain't nobody scared of her. She just mad because Guy n' Tyron be getting fresh with us. Anyway, she ain't coming downstairs. That's how you call a person's bluff when they threaten you. My brother always told me that once people see that you are scared, they will always test you, but when you put them in their place right out the gate, you won't have many problems," Envy responded, sharing what her brother had told her many times before.

"But what if she does come downstairs?" India nervously questioned as if she was shook!

“Then she would’ve been here already. And you and I wouldn’t be discussing this. We would be fighting by now,” Envy explained before laughing. “Plus, I’m not worried about her. All I have to do is call my cousins from Marcy, or wait till my Aunt Promise get here. She’s coming to stay with my mother and Aunt Jasmine for the summer. You already know that my aunt is noooo joke!”

Promise was Mercedes youngest sister and she lived in Fayetteville, NC with Mercedes’ dad, stepmother, and two other sisters, Janet and Ester. Promise was a fighter and was not afraid of anyone; especially if somebody messed with Envy or Jah.

Envy then began to tell India about an incident that happened when they were younger. “India, I remember one time we were on St Marks and this chick named Samantha was chasing Jah around the park. Promise didn’t know that they were playing because Samantha wasn’t smiling. You know how she always plays with Jah like that.

“Anyway, Promise was like, ‘Don’t run, Jah, but he kept on running in circles around the monkey bars. Promise jumped up and grabbed him and said, ‘Didn’t I tell you not to run! Ain’t nobody gonna touch you.’ Samantha said something and Promise gave her the business. It was quick and brutal. When my Aunt Jessica ran over and tried to break it up, Samantha wouldn’t let Promise’s legs go so Jessica started punching her in the face…”

India interrupted, "Oh my goodness, Envy! Jessica is so nice. I didn't know that she's a fighter."

Envy started laughing before responding, "You are stupid, India. But I guess she wanted Samantha to get off of her little sister. She wouldn't let her legs go, so Jessica got her off of her the best way she knew how even though Promise was kicking Samantha all in her face. She eventually let Promise legs go."

"What's good, yal?" The girls were interrupted.

"Nothing much. Chillin', Dee Dee. What you been up to?" They both asked.

"Nothing, I'm good. Yal look cute. Yal better be going to school and not creepin'," Dee Dee joked.

"How you figure? Ain't nobody creepn'," Envy spoke up for the both of them.

"Envy, don't act like I don't be seeing you on Malcom X with David!" Dee Dee followed up.

"Damn! Let me find out you be watching me!" Envy exclaimed before they all started laughing.

"See yal later," Dee Dee responded and the girls kept it moving.

"Envy, I can't stand them fake broads!" India snarled after Dee Dee walked off.

"Me neither. You know one of them is sleeping with David. Because how do she know who I'm down there with? Why is she clocking me?" Envy questioned out loud. "And you know that her homegirl Trent is creepin' with Lay."

Just as the girls reached the corner of Gates and Stuyvesant, they decided to go into the corner store. As they walked into the corner store, Lay walked in right behind them. "What's good, India?"

"On my way to school. What about you, Lay?" India asked.

"I'm out here chillin', getting this money. You know how I do," Lay stated, not knowing that the girls were just talking about him.

"Yea, I know. I just saw your little boo, Dee Dee!" India sarcastically spoke as she rolled her eyes at him.

"Get outta here with that bull! Don't play with me, India. You know that you're my only boo,"

Lay said as he rubbed his fingers through India's pretty hair.

"Hey, Poppy! Can I get a pack of Doublemint, spearmint, Juicy Fruit, and Winterfresh gum, please? And let me get a bagel with cream cheese and jelly," Envy ordered for herself and India being that India was being occupied by Lay. "India, give me your $1.50 for your food."

India dug into her pocket. "Here you go." India handed her the money and sarcastically said, "Envy, didn't we just see Lay's boo?"

"Yep! We sure did see his boo down the block," Envy agreed with India, picking with Lay. So what. Envy always had her girl's back. It didn't matter. Envy paid for the food and the three of them left the store.

"Envy, you need to mind your business because I know that you are lying for your friend," Lay stated as he walked the girls across the street.

"She's not lying, Lay. You know that's your boo!" India shouted. "And you need to come to school sometimes and stop cutting all day!" she added.

"Don't worry about me, India. I'm good. Out here getting this money is better than school," Lay stated as he walked away and the girls went inside of the school building.

The day started with David chasing and feeling up on Envy, nothing but love taps before taking a pack of her gum. He would then go to his class and the girls would go to theirs. They had the same boring teacher, Mr. Givens, so the morning started off slowly. It wasn't until lunch time when the paced picked up. Sixth period lunch was the bomb! Everybody that was somebody ate lunch that period.

"Envy, come here," David requested as he signaled her to come over to him.

Envy walked over to him, "What's up?"

"You are what's up. I'm about to leave school and go chill at Spliff's crib. Are you coming to chill with me?" he asked.

"Are you going by yourself or should I bring somebody?" she curiously asked.

"You know that the whole crew is going to be there, so you can bring whoever you want as long as they are cool," he replied.

"Okay, I'll see what I can do," she responded before walking away. Envy was amped and ready to leave school but she needed a partner in crime.

"Awwwww, look at Envy blushing. She is just so in love with her boo," Izel teased as she laughed and picked on Envy, knowing that she had put Envy on blast and Envy ignored her

Envy had planned on leaving after Mr. Lee's 7th period class. He was an old country man that would cuss any of the children out at any time once they struck his last nerve. His patience was very short. Envy, Izel, India, and Cheyenne all sat at the same table in the back of the class.

"Envy, I'm ready to leave school. It's boring! I just don't feel like being here," India complained, not knowing those were the words Envy needed to hear.

"So what's up? What are you trying to do?" Envy asks.

"We can walk through Malcolm X and see what's poppin' on that end," India suggested.

"Okay, that sounds good. We just have to figure out a way to get out of here," Envy added before they started scheming.

“I’ll ask if I can use the bathroom, then you wait like two minutes and come out,” India suggested and Envy agreed.

“Envy, you know that you don’t need to cut school. Didn’t you just get off of punishment?” Izel asked after reminding Envy of the trouble she’d just gotten out of.

“Izel, shut up! You need to come on and go with us. Don’t worry about my punishment. You rollin’ or what?”

“Yep, I’m rollin. We only have one more period left. I ain’t missing nothing,” Izel stated.

India asked if she could use the restroom and to their surprise, Mr. Lee declined. Okay, plan A didn’t work so it was time for the usual plan B. The girls sat in the back and by the door for moments just like this.

Envy begin the count, “Three, two, one!”

Mr. Lee was turned to the chalkboard and on one, the girls ran out the back door of the classroom. By the time Mr. Lee turned around and reached the back of the class, the girls were already hiding in the girl's bathroom.

"LIL LADIES! IMA WRITE YAL FRESH TAILS UP! YAL ARE GOING TO BE PREGNANT BY THE TIME YAL REACH 15! ALL OF YAL! RUNNING BEHIND THEM DAMN BOYS…" were his last words before slamming the door.

Once the door was closed, the girls knew that it was safe for them to come out of hiding. How did Mr. Lee know what they were up to? They didn't know but they didn't care. Oh well, they broke out anyway. The usual escape route on the Special Ed side was their exit.

Once they reached Malcolm X, India ran into her other shorty, Bezo. She decided to chill with him until it was time to go home. Envy and Izel continued their journey down to Jackie Robinson PJs to check David and 'em, which was right up Izel's alley. She had a shorty over there, too, Little Rommel, who later on in life, discovered that he was her cousin. But that's another story.

"Meanwhile, back at the ranch…"

The girls had reached Halsey and Malcolm X Boulevard when they ran into someone!

"Ayo, Izel, don't that look like Michelle standing in front of the store?" Envy asked, pointing at a girl in her sights.

"Yep, Envy, that is that tramp," Izel responded with disgust.

"Okay, it's my lucky day," Envy stated as she walked up to Michelle.

"Ayo, Michelle, what's good?" was all Envy said before punching Michelle in her face.

Envy beat the brakes off of Michelle. She did it so quickly that Michelle didn't have a chance to fight back. Some older women coming out of the supermarket broke the fight up. After the fight was broken up, the girls continued to Jackie Robinson PJs, thinking that Michelle was going to get her crew.

While they were walking, Envy noticed that David's bowlegged self was walking up the block and the reason she was fighting Michelle crossed her mind. The day Michelle and her crew jumped her, it was over David and in front of him. The thought made Envy want to put it on Michelle again in front of David.

Envy ran up to Michelle again and grabbed a handful of her hair just as Michelle turned around.

Envy didn't sneak Michelle, she just wasn't quick enough and didn't see it coming. Michelle threatened to go get her girl Bubbles. Like Envy gave a damn about Bubbles. Bubbles don't stop any show!

"Come here, you TRICK!" were Envy's words when she snatched Michelle by the hair and yanked her to the ground. Envy dragged her right in front of David. She stomped her out and beat the hell out of her again before David finally broke up the fight.

"CHILL, ENVY! SHE HAD ENOUGH! LOOK AT HER! SHE'S DONE," David yelled as he grabbed Envy off of Michelle. He then turned and yelled at Izel, "LIL' I, GET ENVY AND YAL GO AHEAD BEFORE THE COPS COME!"

Envy and Izel quickly walked away. "Little I" was the name that the Malcolm X crew gave Izel because she was so little. David caught up with them and congratulated Envy on her boxing skills. They walked back to Putnam and met up with India. They filled her in on what happened and headed home. David and Bezo walked the girls to Madison and Stuyvesant then headed back to their hood.

"Envy, thc only reason you beat her like that the second time is because you saw David. I mean, you did her dirty the first round, but once you saw David, you went crazy on her! That poor girl didn't know what to do," Izel stated as she laughed and joked about Michelle trying to grab Envy but not being able to get a hold of her.

"Yep, I sure did. You know that they jumped us on Decatur about a month ago, and I was dead serious about what I was going to do when I caught her. I was going to give her the business, and she knew it, too. That's why she hasn't been to school in a minute. I guess she thought that if she didn't come to school, she wouldn't see me again. Not to mention she tried to go hard because David was there and she's taking off them panties for him! That's the part that pisses me off the most. Izel, you know if David and them wouldn't have broken the fight up that night, they were really going to hurt me. Too bad they can't fight so there was no real damage done," Envy explained, still excited from the fight.

"I wish that I was there," India added.

"Please, India, because you weren't going to do a thang!" Izel sarcastically shot back.

"Whatever, Izel. I sure didn't hear about you doing anything, either!" India spat after Izel tried to play her.

"Please, I always do something! I'm always there. You never there and if you are there, you never do anything. SO DON'T PLAY WITH ME!" Izel yelled.

"Whatever, Izel, because I wasn't even talking to you. I was talking to my friend Envy!" India continued as she rolled her eyes and pointing at Envy.

"India, don't make me punch you in your face!"

"Well then do it! Ain't nobody scared of you," India boasted.

As Izel went to punch India, Envy jumped in between, "YAL NEED TO CHILL OUT! YAL LOOK REAL STUPID RIGHT NOW!"

"No, Envy! You know that I can't stand her! She always has something smart to say and you're always saving her," Izel complained after expressing her dislike for India.

"Alright, Izel. Here comes your bus. Go ahead and catch it and call me when you get home," Envy said, changing the subject and stopping her two friends from fighting.

Izel rolled her eyes and hopped on the bus while Envy and India continued their journey. Envy knew that India wasn't a fighter but she sure did talk plenty of trash to Envy and whoever else, but wouldn't swat a fly or bust a grape, so Envy would always save her.

They had finally reached their block. Envy's building was first so they said their goodbyes and departed. When Envy got upstairs, Jah and Corey were in the crib chilln'.

"What's up, Blacko?" Jah stated as he hugged Envy.

"Nothing much, chillin'. I just had a fight."

"With who?" Jah eyes widened as he asked.

"Remember that chick that I told you that jumped me like a month ago on Decatur and Malcolm X but she never came back to school? Well, her… She finally came back to school," Envy lied.

She knew that she had to because she couldn't tell Jah that she ditched school, especially to go on Malcolm X. Jah would've fried her. Being that neither one of their fathers was around, Jah took on the role of being Envy's dad.

"Did you win?" Jah asked.

"Yep! I sure did," Envy confidently answered.

"Well, that's all that matters. I thought that I might have to give you some more lessons," Jah responded seriously.

He used to give Envy one hour a day boxing lessons when they had time. And when he wasn't there, Mercedes gave her self-defense lessons. Not that either of them was a boxer or self-defense instructor, but it worked for Envy

"Envy, you are always fighting. Somebody is going to whip that butt one day," Corey said, jumping into the conversation.

"Oh, shut up, Corey, and mind your business. I bet your girl can't beat me," Envy barked at Corey.

"I don't have a girl. But I bet that I can beat you," Corey spat back, joking with Envy.

"So what up, Corey? Put your money where your mouth is," Envy said before throwing her hands up in a fighting position like a professional boxer.

As Corey stood up, Jah put him in a chokehold from behind.

"OH. WOW! Yal jumping me?" Corey stated as they all laughed. "Get off me. Jah! I thought you were my man."

"Nobody messes with my baby sista!" Jah responded with the mean face and voice before letting Corey go.

"I'm not messing with yal. The Johnson kids love to jump people. But Envy, Ima catch you outside by yourself. Watch. Right, when the Johnny pump is on, too, and Ima drench your skinny butt!" Corey threatened as he laughed.

The truth was that Envy and Corey had a thing for each other and when Jah wasn't around, they would do their flirting and sometimes smooch, but they knew that Jah couldn't find out. The three of them talked laughed and played the game until Envy got tired and went to bed.

Luckily, Mercedes didn't find out about what went down with Envy, so the rest of the school week went by pretty smoothly. No punishment for Envy, so she was able to hang out a little bit during the following weekend. And there was no telling what mischievous activities Envy would find herself in.

Chapter 6

ADDITION TO THE FAMILY

Mercedes received an emergency phone call from a social worker stating that her brother Jeff and his woman Sylvia were arrested for drug use and their children were being held at the hospital until they could find placement for them. Jeff asked if they could call Mercedes to see if she would take the children. The plan was to be temporary until they got themselves together.

Mercedes took in the children and eventually the parents, too. It was her worst mistake because it became a conflict of interest. Jeff and Sylvia thought because they were the biological parents, whatever assistance that Mercedes received for the kids, they deserved half. Mercedes wasn't having it. So that created problem #1.

Then, they were drug addicts, so the running in and out, different people ringing the doorbell at whatever hour of the night and early in the morning was a no-go. It was no lifestyle for Mercedes and her children. Sylvia went as far as to take Envy with her to buy crack and would even smoke it in front of her.

One time, Sylvia allowed Envy to chill in the staircase with her and explained step by step how the whole crack-smoking process goes. She had a glass cup, a piece of aluminum foil, a lighter and a small piece of what look like a white rock. She then placed the aluminum foil on top of the glass and the rock cocaine on top of the aluminum foil. What she did next scared Envy. Sylvia began to act as if she was sucking the crack through the glass as she held the lit lighter underneath the glass. And when she stopped lighting it, her eyes grew bigger.

Envy tried to keep it a secret but Mercedes had it to where Envy could tell her anything, especially things like that. After a while, Mercedes couldn't put up with it. Jeff had gone back to jail and Sylvia was not getting better at all. She made it worse when she went on her crack binges because Mercedes needed her help with the boys. She would leave for days and weeks at a time and it hurt the boys because they loved their mother dearly. They would cry for hours and have temper tantrums that Mercedes and Envy had to deal with.

Earl wasn't as bad as Dre, but it was still hard for Mercedes to bond with the boys because as soon as she got them calm and the way that she wanted them, here came Sylvia for a couple of days, only to leave again. Therefore, Mercedes decided to adopt Earl and Dre and sent Sylvia on her way for good.

One day, while Mercedes had taken the boys to visit their social worker at the agency, Envy had a surprise visitor. Guess who?

"Envy, I have a meeting at the agency. I'll be back around seven. Here're a couple of dollars to get something to eat. I don't mind if you have company but don't have that music blasting," Mercedes instructed Envy before leaving.

"Okay, Ma. I won't."

"Thanks, see you later. Love you," Mercedes said before giving Envy a kiss goodbye.

Envy then kissed Earl and Dre before leaving. Dre was Envy's baby. He was just the cutest little baby with his thick hair and he was so sweet. Dre only wanted his mother so he was a little difficult to deal with at times. They left and Envy was chilling. About an hour later, the intercom rang.

Envy answered, "Who is it?"

"It's me, Corey. Is Jah there?" his voice came through the intercom system.

"No he's not and I don't know where he is," she answered.

"Aright, buzz me in."

Envy buzzed the door with a confused expression on her face. She wondered why he would want to be buzzed in after she told him that her brother wasn't home. About five minutes later, the doorbell rang.

"What, Corey?! Didn't I tell you that my brother is not here?"

"Shut up, Envy. How about I came to see you?" he stated in a sarcastic manner.

"See me for what?" Envy responded with a puzzled look plastered on her face.

"Who's here with you?"

"Nobody, why?" she responded, continuing the cat and mouse game.

"Can I come in?"

Envy was hesitant but, after looking at the clock and noticing that it was only 4 o'clock, decided to let him in. Her mother wouldn't be home until seven and if Jah came, she could say that Corey just got there looking for him.

"Envy, you know that I like you. I don't know why you be frontin'," Corey stated as they made their way into the living room.

"How am I supposed to know that you like me?" she asked with the biggest blush on her face.

"You can tell by the way that I look at you and lick my lips that I want you. This is not a regular like. A brother doesn't just do this to everybody," Corey stated.

"Oh, my gosh, Corey. I really did not know that you like me like that. It's not like we can make any moves. You know that my brother is not going for that," Envy explained, acting as if she didn't know how Corey felt.

"The whole thing about it is Jah don't have to know anything. What we do is between us," Corey tried to rationalize with a manipulative smirk on his face.

"I don't know, Corey. I have to give this situation some thought. I feel funny betraying my brother's trust."

"Envy, how is that betraying him? He never told you that you couldn't mess with me, right? That was never a rule of his."

"I know, Corey, but I know better."

Before Envy could finish her sentence, Corey grabbed her face and quickly threw his tongue inside of her mouth and she didn't put up a fight. Envy didn't know how to kiss but she embraced Corey and did something that day! From that moment, Envy and Corey became secret lovers. Corey chilled with her for a little while and they both enjoyed each other's company alone. Laughing, play fighting, and smooching was all they did for the past hour. After a while, Corey left and Envy cleaned herself up to get the smell of saliva and Corey off of her before her mother or Jah came home. In Envy's eyes, Jah and Mercedes could detect anything.

Once Envy was clean, she decided to walk over to the Chinese restaurant to get her favorite, shrimp and broccoli smothered on top of white rice. The front of 685 was crowded because of the nice summer weather. Everybody and their momma were out. The rowdy boys were in front of the building making noise by cracking jokes on everything moving and Envy was no exception.

"What's up, SMOKEEEY?" one of the guys said (in the Spanish guy from Friday's voice) and they all burst out laughing.

"Stop playing with me, yal. My name is not Smokey," Envy responded as she passed them.

"SHUT UP, SMOKEEEEY!" the guy yelled.

"I'm not even going to feed into yal low life losers' jokes. Kiss my black Smokey butt!" Envy popped back while rolling her eyes before walking across the street.

The guys were Envy's schoolmates. Some of them lived in her building and some lived a block over on Quincy Street. A few of them just came through to hang out with the crew. They named her Smokey because of her dark complexion, a puff of smoke, as they called it. They also nicknamed India "Essay" because she was Spanish, so teasing them was an everyday routine for the boys.

Envy looked down the block at Stop 1, the corner store, which was full of the latest flavas, and so was the other corner store, Munchies. On a nice day like this, Envy would usually get India, Kara, or Izel to walk from hood to hood to check out the scenery but this day was different.

Envy was full of desire for Corey. All she wanted to do was sit in the crib and think of what took place between her and Corey. Was Corey being honest with her about his feelings, and how could they get around Jah if they started a relationship?

Envy finally made it to the Chinese restaurant but before she could walk in, guess who was standing there full of compliments?

"Hey, pretty, you look nice. You are so pretty, with all of that hair and pretty skin," Crackhead Dawn complimented with a noticeable knot on her head.

"Thanks, Dawn," Envy replied and kept it moving, knowing what Dawn wanted.

Dawn followed her. "Pretty, do you got a quarter?"

"Wait a minute, Dawn. Let me order my food then I will see what I have left," Envy said politely.

"Okay, Pretty." Best to believe Dawn followed right behind Envy to get whatever Envy had for her.

After Envy paid for her food, she gave Dawn a whole dollar! That was like Christmas for Dawn because she hugged and thanked Envy so much, you would've never thought that she'd never seen a dollar before in life.

After her food was done, Envy went back upstairs, ate her food and popped in her Mary J Cd.

She began to sing, “For so long I waited for the chance to be with you until I was through, baaaby… in my dreams, I take you by the hands in a house on the beach, making love or just laxingggg.”

“Damn, Envy, why are you in here blasting music like this?” Jah asked after catching her in the living room with her eyes closed and acting like she was singing into a mic.

“Oh shoot, Jah! Don’t scare me like that again!” she blurted out in a state of shock.

Jah turned the music off. For a minute, Envy was about to complain but once Jah put *Super Mario Brothers* in, it became a challenge to see who could beat the master. Of course, Jah won because if Envy came close to winning, he would either distract or manipulate her, so it was a no-win situation for her.

“Hello, my children, I’m home!! I’m so tired. What’s new?” Mercedes asked as she kicked off her shoes and relaxed her feet after sitting in her recliner. “Envy, run some bath water for Earl and Dre.”

“But Maaaaa…”

Mercedes cut her off, “Don’t but ‘ma’ me! Go do what I said, now!” Mercedes ordered as she pointed toward the bathroom.

Things within the family were going smoothly. No punishment for Envy, and Jah was cool. Ty's death had taken a toll on him but he was beginning to live the life of a gangster.

Envy went and ran the bath water just as a her mother instructed. Afterwards, she wrapped her hair and went to bed with thoughts of Corey on her mind until she fell asleep.

Chapter 7

THE LAST DAY OF JUNIOR HIGH SCHOOL

The last day of school was poppin'! No work, no order, and everyone found out what high school they were accepted to. Mr. Givens' class was wide open. After calling names and giving out report cards, Mr. Givens finally reached Envy's name and told her that she was accepted to Paul Robeson High School.

Envy was excited because her new school would be right across the street from Albany PJs and around the corner from St. Marks. It was also a school for business, which was Envy's major! Envy couldn't ask for anything better.

"India, what school is you going to?" Envy asks.

"I'm going to Sarah J. Hale," India responded.

"Izel, what school is you going to?" Envy asks.

“I’m going right to The High (Boys and Girls High School). What about you, Envy?” Izel questioned.

“I’m going to Robe. Aww, man! I’m gonna miss my friends. None of us are going to the same school,” Envy whined.

“That don’t mean nothing, Envy. We will never be apart,” India declared to her friend.

“Yea, I guess you’re right.”

“Yea, girl. You better stay in touch! I will be close by. We will be right in Albany PJs!” Izel stated as she laughed.

“Yes, girl, you already know!” Envy responded.

After assembly, there was an early release. Too bad Envy didn’t get to walk across the stage due to cutting school and multiple fights. It didn’t matter to Envy as long as she got promoted!!

Envy, India, Izel, and Cheyenne went and chilled on Malcolm X. Boulevard. Being that it was only 11:30 when they were released, they had a long day ahead of them.

Once they got on the Boulevard, Izel copped a bag of weed but no one ever knew she smoked.

"Listen yal, it's the last day of school. I'm about to get bent!! IT'S A CELEBRATIONNN!" Izel yelled.

"Trick! When did you start smokin'?" Envy asked.

"I been smoking. I just didn't let nobody know," Izel responded while smelling the small sack of green.

"Oh, that's what you do with your Sumner Project friends, huh?" Envy sarcastically asked.

"Girrrl, please! I know that you don't smoke so why would I bring that to you?" Izel got smart right back with Envy. "But if you want to celebrate, let's get it poppin'! Forget the small talk. Now you know!"

Cheyenne jumped in, "I'm down!"

"Cheyenne, you smoke, too?" Envy asked, surprised at her willingness.

"Not really but I tried it before, and today is celebration day. What's poppin'?"

“Well, let’s get it poppin’! I’m down, too,” Envy finally agreed.

They went to 305 Park and began their journey. Even India’s scary self hit the blunt.

“Yooo, I think that I’m high,” Envy stated as she burst out in laughter.

“Me, too, and I’m scared. Why are these people looking at me like that?!” India asked, acting all paranoid.

“Yal better not start trippin’!” Izel warned.

“Whaaaat if we are high? What are we supposed to do? This is not a normal feeling for us,” Envy humbly questioned.

“Suck it up and chill,” Cheyenne replied.

“Yal are smokers, we are not, so what do we know?” India asked.

“Yal can just chill out, relax and enjoy the feeling,” Izel replied with her eyes half-closed.

The girls went and chilled at Cheyenne’s crib because her aunt was not home. First, they asked for all of her goodies, then they wanted to dance. They laughed at everything and then they all became paranoid. They began to think that somebody else was in the house because they began hearing noises. After acting silly for a while, the girls dozed off to sleep. They were passed out when Cheyenne's aunt came in. She woke them up and sent them home.

As they walked the streets of Bed-Stuy, everything seemed so brand new and amazing to the girls. The people even looked different.

"Hey, Izel, you are like 2 feet tall with a big head," Envy joked as she pointed and laughed at her.

"Shut up, Blacky, with your big lips," Izel immediately snapped back and started laughing.

"Whatever, Smurf," Envy replied.

"And India, don't laugh because you look like an Arab with your thin ponytail," Envy continued to joke.

"Shut up, Envy! I'm scared! I feel funny and these people are looking at me like I'm crazy," India said, feeling paranoid.

"You better drink some milk. You can't go home like that. Ms. Linda is going to know that you're high," Izel stated, finally having something nice and positive to say to India for the first time in her life. "Oh snap, yal! There goes my bus. Ima catch up with yal later. Envy, call me," Izel spoke quickly as she jetted for the bus.

Envy and India had reached Gates Ave.

"Envy, can you walk me to Munchies to get a small thing of milk?" India asked.

"Only if you wait with me for Earl and Dre to get off the school bus."

"Okay, I'll wait. That way my high can cool down," India compromised.

The girls walked to Munchies high as hell. In their minds, everyone seemed to be looking at them funny. The girls felt like they were dreaming because nothing seemed real. When the girls reached Munchies, they ran into Bob Kat, another well-known neighborhood crackhead. Bob Kat was the realest.

"What are yal doing looking like Chipmunks?" Bob Kat asked and the sight of her two missing front teeth made Envy and India burst out laughing. "Oh yeah, yal girls are on something. I'm telling yal mothers, too! I know what's wrong with yal. Bob Kat ain't no fool and I was born at night but not last night!" Bob Kat continued before leaving the store.

The girls were giggling really hard, not only at what she said but also how she looked! Especially in the state of mind that they were in. They would never disrespect Bob Kat or any other neighborhood crackhead. It was always love. India purchased her milk and the girls left the store. India drank her milk while they were walking.

By the time they reached the building, the bus was pulling up. Envy got the boys off the bus, said goodbye to India, then went upstairs. As soon as Envy reached her apartment, she hit the kitchen and made two bowls of cereal, then a jelly bagel. She took care of her munchies with some other snacks then slept the rest of her high away.

Earl and Dre were good kids. They knew to make a peanut butter and jelly sandwich and sit tight and watch cartoons until either Envy woke up or Mercedes came home. Eventually, they fell asleep as well.

Around 5:30 in the evening, Mercedes came home.

"Envy, Envy, wake up. I'm home."

Envy was a light sleeper so it didn't take much for her to wake up. "Hey, Ma, I'm up," Envy moaned as she sat up on the sofa and stretched.

"Why are all of yal knocked out so early? Yal must've had a long day in school," Mercedes stated as she entered the kitchen to put away a few groceries.

"Yea, I did. Today we found out what high school we are going to, then they let us have a field day all day," Envy stated, mixing some facts with fiction. Envy's high had not worn off yet so she was trying to play it off as if she was alert when, in reality, Envy was really worn out and tired at the same time.

"Envy, wake those boys up. They will not sleep all day then stay up all night. I don't care if it is the last day of school," Mercedes stated.

As Envy headed to wake the boys, the intercom rang.

"I GOT IT, MA. WHO IS IT?" Envy yelled as she pressed the talk button and spoke into the intercom.

"IT'S ME, SYLVIA," the unwanted voice of Sylvia came through the intercom.

Envy rolled her eyes, buzzed the door and then kept it moving.

"I wonder what she wants. I hope she's coming to surprise me and say that she got herself an apartment and she's taking the boys for the summer," Mercedes hopefully spoke.

A few minutes later, the doorbell rang and it was Sylvia. Envy opened the door.

"Hey, Envy, what's up?" Sylvia asked.

"Nothing much, I'm doing well," Envy mumbled, still trying to shake off her high.

"Hey, Mercedes, how you doing?" Sylvia said enthusiastically.

"I'm fine. How about yourself?" Mercedes politely responded.

"I'm doing well. I was over here with Carol and wanted to stop by to tell the boys my good news."

Carol was Kara's mom and another well-respected neighborhood crackhead and so were her two brothers, Steve and Al. Carol was Sylvia's partner in crime. They would go on binges together while Ms. Anne, Kara's grandmother, would be left to care for her. And when Al went on his binges, Ms. Anne also had to care for his son Jimmy, who was born with AIDS. He wasn't supposed to live past 2 years old but he was 7, so that shows the devil is a liar!

The boys came running into the living room and after giving their mother a hug, Sylvia blurted out, "Well, boys! Mommy is having a baby, and hopefully, this is my girl."

The boys didn't really understand what she was talking about. But she was just that weird that she would really expect for them to understand and show some real emotion behind that.

"Girl, are you serious! You can't even take care of the two you have," Mercedes was not biting her tongue at all because she really couldn't stand Sylvia.

After Sylvia moved out, she went around the hall and told Carol and Ms. Ann all of Mercedes' business. She talked about her and her kids like dogs and even told major lies. Mercedes found out after Ms. Ann called herself flipping on Mercedes for talking about how she'd done Sylvia. After putting Ms. Ann in her place, Mercedes never wanted Sylvia back in her presence. However, Mercedes had a soft spot for the kids and for the sake of the boys, she allowed Sylvia to continue to visit.

Again, Sylvia blurted out, “Yes, I know but this is my last one and I’m done. I know that I have to get myself together so that I can get my boys, too. I miss them! Can the boys walk with me to the store?”

“As long as you don’t have them out too late,” Mercedes reluctantly answered.

“Okay, I promise I’ll bring them right back!”

Sylvia got the boys together and they left. As soon as Sylvia left out the door, Mercedes jumped on the phone and calls Jessica and then they called Jasmine on three-way.

“Guess what, yal?” Mercedes started off.

“Girl, what?” They both asked.

“Ol’ Sylvia got the nerve to be pregnant again!”

“Oh no she ain’t!” Jessica blurted out.

"Whaaaat?" Jasmine replied to the news before Mercedes continued.

"Yes, and she comes up in here like she got such great news and everyone supposed to jump up and down and congratulate her! She gets me sick!" Mercedes complained.

"She ain't gonna do nothing but let this one get taken by the system just like the rest of them," Jessica stated.

"And it might not be Jeff's because ain't he locked up? How many months is she?" Jasmine questioned.

"It might not be his. You know she's out there doing everybody for crack. And I didn't give her a chance to say how many months she is. I just looked at her like she was crazy. She could tell that I wasn't happy to hear that, so she got them kids and got the hell out of here!" Mercedes explained before laughing.

"I don't even know why she came back around if you did her so wrong. What, she didn't think that you would ever find out all of what she said?" Jasmine asked.

"All she does is go around there and play pitiful so that she can have a place to stay. I guess she figures if she talks about me and makes me look bad, people would feel sorry for her."

Envy was tired of eavesdropping on her mother's convo so she decided to go into her room and listen to some music. She turned the radio on Hot 97 and her song "No Scrubs" by TLC was playing.

"I don't want no scrub; a scrub is a guy that can't get no love from me…"

"Remix...Noooooooo, OOH, PIGEONS," Envy yelled as she listened to the song.

"A pigeon is a girl who is walking by my rimmed up blue, brand new sparkling five, her feet hurt so you know she wants a ride…"

Envy had never heard the rebuttal before so that tune caught her attention. She had to call somebody to see if they heard that "No Scrubs" remix. She went running out of the room toward the phone. She heard her mother talking loud and laughing, which made her realize that the phone was not available. Envy knew that once Mercedes got on the phone with her sisters, Jessica and Jasmine, it was going to be an 8-hour gossip session!

The doorbell rang and Envy ran to answer it, wondering who it was because no one had rung the intercom downstairs. Envy looked through the peephole and then opened the door for Sylvia.

"I'm just bringing the boys back."

"Oh, okay," Envy responded as the boys ran past her.

"Envy, Kara asked for you. She wanted to know if you can come around the corner."

"Okay, wait for me. I'm about to walk around there with you," Envy stated. "MA, I'M GOING AROUND THE CORNER TO KARA'S."

"OKAY, YOU BETTER NOT COME IN LATE," Mercedes yelled back from her bedroom. Mercedes really didn't care to know what Envy was talking about, being that she was so into her conversation.

Sylvia gave the boys their snacks and sat them in front of the T.V. before letting Mercedes know they were there, then she and Envy left.

Once they were in the hallway, Sylvia stopped next to the staircase doorway and said, "Wait a minute, Envy. Come with me in the staircase for a moment. I have to do something."

She and Sylvia sat on the steps. Envy already knew what time it was! It was grouse! Envy watched for a moment before asking in a disgusted tone, "Why do you smoke that?"

"Because it helps me, Envy. With my kids being gone, your uncle in jail, me being pregnant, and I'm homeless. It's hard for me to deal with all of this stress on my own. And this relaxes me mentally," Sylvia made excuses for not being about her business. She was making excuses for letting the drugs take over her life, and Envy knew it. Envy couldn't stand what Sylvia was doing and saying.

"No, Sylvia. I think that you are making excuses. The high helps you forget about your problems, but that doesn't fix them. Really, it just makes you not care about life. That's how I see it. And my mother has to take care of your kids while you out here living scot-free getting high," Envy scolded Sylvia before walking out of the staircase, disgusted that Sylvia would actually do that in front of her again! Envy was also a little jealous that she had to share her mother's time with Sylvia's kids.

"ENVY, I'M SORRY! PLEASE DON'T TELL YOUR MOTHER!" Sylvia yelled and they were the last words that Envy heard before the staircase door slammed behind her.

At that point, Envy realized her own strengths and weaknesses. Sylvia thought because Envy was young, she didn't mind or understand what was really going on. That's how it always happens. It takes someone to introduce another to the drug just off of a tryout, and then the world has another crackhead. Thank God Envy was not weak minded toward everything because from that one incident, she could have lost her life to crack.

However, Envy was not as strong when dealing with her own peers. "Peer pressure is a mother…" But there were enough crackheads in the hood for Envy to know and see that was not her destiny. The chronic only gives you the munchies, makes you giggle and fatigued. At worst it might make you have a panic attack and a little paranoid. Now if the cannabis oil in the chronic doesn't respond right to the cannabis receptors in your brain, it can make you go crazy, but um... That crack had them weak and doing something strange for some change.

All drugs sound unhealthy to me, but you live and you learn fast when growing up a chick in Brooklyn!

Chapter 8

SUMMER TIME IN THE CITY

Once school was out, the summer season hit hard. That was usual for BK. Most of the kids were looking forward to getting a job with the Summer Youth Program, the live concerts at Tompkins Park, block parties the hood way and basketball tournaments were poppin' at Soul Hole (44 Park)! Whenever someone wasn't throwing a bus ride to Great Adventures, most kids went to Coney Island. No school! WHAT! This was the best time of the year!

"Envy, here. You got some mail. I think it's from the Summer Youth Program. Hurry, open it and see what it says." Mercedes was excited as she handed Envy her mail.

Envy opened the letter and chose to read it out loud. "Dear Envy Johnson, you have been selected to participate in our Summer Youth Program…"

That's all Envy needed to hear, read, and see. She went on to read the date and time for her appointment. She was excited to find out that her appointment was the very next day at 9 A.M. She was thrilled to have her first job. It felt good for her to not have to ask her mother for anything. She would be able to buy whatever she wanted at whatever price, as long as she could afford it. And yes, she started calculating paychecks immediately. She began to vision her summer wardrobe, and she hadn't even gotten the job yet. Lol. It's the principle.

Envy couldn't wait to tell anyone that crossed her path that she was getting a job. First, she had to call India. She ran to the phone and dialed India's number.

India answered on the second ring, "Hey, Envy, I was just about to call you. What's up?"

"I was calling to tell you that they picked me for a summer job…"

"ME TOO! I gotta go tomorrow at 9 o'clock in the morning," India interrupted before Envy could finish.

"Oh, that's good! We can go together," Envy suggested.

"Do you have to go to Sheepshead Bay?" India asked.

"Yea," Envy responded before reading the address off to India. They agreed that they had the same appointment at the same time and place.

"Okay, Envy, I'm about to come over there."

"Okay, come on," Envy replied and they hung up. Next, Envy dialed Izel. "Hey, Ms. Chel, this is Envy. Is Izel home?"

"Envy, I know your voice and no, she's not. She had to go pick Riah up from daycare."

"Okay, thanks. Can you have her call me?"

"Yes, I'll have her call you when she gets back, and yal better not be up to no good."

"No, we're not, Ms. Chel. I just wanted to talk to her," Envy responded after a devilish giggle.

"Okay, she'll call you later," Ms. Chel replied and they hung up.

Finally, Envy called Kara. "Hey, Ms. Anne. Is Kara in?"

"Yea, hol' on. Kara, here, it's your buddy Envy."

"What's up, Envy? Whatchu doing?" Kara questioned when she got on the phone.

"Nothing much. GUESS WHAT, KARA!?" Envy asked excitedly.

"You sound excited. What?" Kara responded.

"I GOT PICKED FOR A SUMMER YOUTH JOB! I'M GETTING PAID THIS SUMMER!" Envy yelled through the phone.

"Envy, you got picked for a summer yummy? ME, TOO!" Kara responded, sharing her good news.

"Oh my gosh! Congratulations! When do you have to go to your appointment?"

"Thank you, and I gotta go Wednesday at 10 o'clock," Kara said and her words disappointed Envy.

"Aww, damn. I thought they probably gave you the same day as me and India. We both got appointments tomorrow at 9," Envy continued.

"I'm mad. How did you get one for tomorrow?" Kara asks.

"Don't hate! Where do you have to go, anyway?" Envy asks.

"My appointment is in Brownsville. And besides, I'm going with my boo P.J. Me and him put in our applications together. And you know that I don't like your friend. I'm glad that I'm not going with her."

"Kara, please. You don't have no reason not to like India. She's done nothing to you," Envy defended India.

"Envy, you know that she gives me stink looks. She thinks that I like David," Kara explained and Envy sucked her teeth before responding.

"How, Kara, when she knows that you go out with P.J.?" Envy asked.

"Well, I don't know what her problem is but I'd rather not deal with her. That's your friend. But do you have to wear black and white to your interview?" Kara quickly changed the subject.

"Yes, I do, but I don't have anything to wear. The only black and white that I have is winter clothes," Envy complained while looking through her closet.

“That’s my problem, too. Do you wanna ride with me to Centuries?” Kara asks.

“I have to ask my mother. You know how she be tripping. As a matter fact, I’m going to tell her that you will buy me something, then she might let me go, knowing that I need something to wear for the interview. I’m going to tell her that we are walking to Graham Ave instead of going all the way to Manhattan,” Envy said, coming up with a scheme as usual.

“Damn, Envy! You stay with a story. You always come up with a quick one, but call me back and let me know the deal,” Kara stated before hanging up the phone with Envy.

Ring! Ring!

The intercom sounded off moments later.

“WHO IS IT?” Mercedes yelled into the intercom.

“It’s me, Auntie!”

“Me, who?” Mercedes asked, knowing that it was India. She just had to pick with her.

“It’s me, India, Auntie! Stop playing,”

Mercedes giggled and buzzed the door.

Envy was stuck on stupid because she just told Kara she would ride with her before India showed up. When India visited Envy, sometimes she didn't leave till after 12 A.M. Envy had to figure out something quick.

Envy thought, *Which one would benefit me more? Chilling with India or rolling with Kara to get her things?* Come on people, you do the math.

India knocked on the door. Envy knew who it was so she opened it. India walked in all loud, "ENVY, I'M SO HAPPY FOR US! WE GETTING JOBS! I'M WAKING UP EARLY TOMORROW!"

"ME, TOO! I'm buying this, I'm buying that..." Envy went on to fantasize about her summer wardrobe again.

India interrupted, "Walk me to the store. I gotta get my mother a hero and a box of Newports."

Envy was hesitant at first because she knew that she and Kara had other plans. Envy was the type that never wanted to disappoint any of her friends or family for the other. Each of them wanted their own special time with her and would get really upset if she denied them for the other. Between Kara, India,

Chelsea, Izel, Beverly, Nay, and Taya, she was bound to upset someone. Chelsea was her baby and Bev was like her sister.

"Wait, let me get my shoes," Envy finally replied.

"Envy, where did you get those Timberland shoe boots from? And when did you get them?" India asks.

"My mother got them yesterday from 4 Kix on Graham Ave."

"I like those. Auntie, why you ain't buy me none?" India asked while admiring Envy's boots.

"I barely had enough for those, but next time Ima get you a pair. Wait till the first," was Mercedes favorite line.

"Come on, India. I'm ready," Envy stated before the girls left the apartment and headed for the store.

"Envy, you know that I'm scared of the elevator. I'm taking the stairs. I'll meet you on the first floor."

“India, you still scared of the elevator? You got stuck in it last year sometime! Get over it already,” Envy stated as she rolled her eyes at India.

“I don’t care what you say. I’m not getting on that elevator! You don’t know how I felt. It was like I was closed in and couldn’t breathe. My heart was pounding. I can’t take that feeling,” India complained before walking toward the staircase.

“India, you are such a drama queen! You are a freakin’ mess. Why all of that, huh, India? Why not just admit that you are scared?” Envy sarcastically stated.

“Because it’s not that I’m scared…,”

“Just come on. I’ll walk with you down the steps,” Envy interrupted after sucking her teeth.

They went through the back staircase and as they were jogging down the first flight of stairs, something big and hairy ran across their path and startled the girls.

“OH MY GOD!” they screamed after backing up and grabbing one another.

“WHAT IS THAT, INDIA!?”

"I DON'T KNOW! I'M NOT GOING TO LOOK!" India stated.

"SEE, THAT'S WHY I SHOULD HAVE TAKEN THE ELEVATOR. NOW LET'S GO CATCH THE ELEVATOR FROM THIS FLOOR!" Envy demanded afraid to continue down the stairs.

"Wait a minute, Envy. I think it's gone. We scared it away."

The girls stood quietly for about 5 seconds and heard nothing. The coast was clear; so they thought. As soon as they went running down to the next flight, the biggest RAT ever ran from underneath a paper bag and in their direction. Both of the girls were knocking each other down to get out of that staircase. They were screaming and jumping all around until they were out of the staircase.

They finally made their way out of the third floor exit. They were running so fast that Envy forgot all about the elevator. They ran around the corner of the hallway to the front staircase. They made their way down the front staircase and through the doors before they stopped to catch their breath and burst out laughing. The incident really tickled their funny bones.

As they were laughing, a voice yelled out, "YALS GET YALS BUTTS OUT OF HERE!" as

Brother came walking from the upper flight of steps, upset that they'd interrupted his crack session.

Being that they were already shaken up, they took off running as fast as they can down the last two flights of steps. Finally, they made it outside. They continued to laugh as hard as they could. Envy almost pissed on herself. They had to stop and sit on the bench in the courtyard for five minutes in order to pull themselves together.

"India, that was so scary but funny at the same time. If somebody was watching us just now… Oh, my gosh! They would've had a good laugh!"

"No, Envy, I'm scared for real! Brother could've raped us. You know he's a rapist?" India asked, still trying to catch her breath.

"Here you go with the extra stuff. Well, at least we are safe. I was more scared of the rat. Did you see how thick it was?" Envy asked.

"I'm scared of the rat, too, but Brother could have done more harm," India stated.

Brother was another neighborhood crackhead. He spent most of his time getting drunk, high and getting into fights with everybody. Brother stayed with a busted lip, knot over his eye, black eye and all of that good stuff. Before he'd let the drugs ruin his life, he was a boxer. So when he got wasted, he thought that he was the old person.

"Come on, let's keep it moving. What store are you getting her sandwich from?" Envy asked.

"Let's go to Stop 1. You know that they make the best sandwiches," India stated.

The girls walked across the street to Stop 1. India ordered the sandwich. "Hey poppy. Let me get a salami and cheese hero with lettuce, onions, salt, pepper, vinegar and oil on some Italian bread."

Poppy began making the hero as the girls walked off to get drinks and other stuff. Poppy and 'em would never harm their food, which was why they felt cool walking off instead of watching him like they would at another store. Everybody had a sandwich from Stop 1 and ain't nobody dropped dead yet.

The girls paid for their things and left the store.

"Envy, I'm not going back in your building. It scared me enough for today. I will see you tomorrow," India laughed but was dead serious.

"No, I walked you to the store, now you have to walk me upstairs!" Envy picked at India.

"And if I walk you upstairs, who is going to walk me back down? I don't think so," India responded as they stood in front of Envy's building.

"Forget you, idiot. Bye," Envy stated as she rang Kara's bell for Kara to meet her on the elevator.

Kara and Envy met and the plan was in full effect. After about 10 minutes of prep talk from Mercedes, Envy and Kara were on their way to Century 21, a store in Manhattan that was poppin'. Envy loved Centuries because she could find anything from classy to sassy to hood. Century 21 sold all of the latest name brand clothing. Envy could go Guess or Versace, Roca Wear or Moschino, NBA jean suits to Roberto Cavalli or Dolce Gabbana. They sold it all.

The girls walked to Gates and Broadway to catch the J train to Manhattan. Once they reached Centuries, it was clothing heaven for them. They went straight to the 3rd floor. The 2nd floor was poppin', too, but that was the regular urban wear section. As soon as they reached the 3rd floor, Envy noticed some black slack-looking stretchy Versace capris. She just had to have them.

"OOOOOH, Kara, check these out!" Envy said, admiring the Versace capris.

"Those are cute, Envy, and they look like they will fit nice on you. How much are those?" Kara asked.

"I'm about to try them on. They want a buck 20 for these," Envy stated.

"Well if Centuries want $120, then what's the original price?" Kara questioned as Envy looked for the original price.

"Whoa! The original price is $350.00!" Envy replied, shocked at the original price. "I'm about to try these on. Come with me to the fitting room."

The girls went into the fitting room and, as usual, the line was long as ever. Envy didn't care so she waited patiently. Finally, she was able to enter a fitting room. Envy had four pieces of clothing in her hand and Kara had about seven pieces.

"Excuse me, ma'am. How many pieces do you have?" the young looking female clerk asked Envy.

"I have 4," Envy answered.

For some reason, the clerk gave Envy a tag for 3 pieces. Envy felt that it was meant for her to have these capris. However, she didn't have the money for them. Envy tried them on and they fit perfectly! The fit around her booty gave it that extra thickness, and the leg part had a loose fit just the way Envy liked them. Not a bell bottom but not a skinny leg fit, either. They were just right!

Once Envy tried the pants on, she couldn't take them off. She just had to have them. They were made for her. Kara was in the room next to Envy.

"Kara, look. How do these fit?" Envy asked when she stepped out of the fitting room.

"Yes, son, those fit bangin'! Look how they fit your butt. David is going to really be starvin' when he lay eyes on you in those!" Kara stated and that's all Envy needed to hear.

After about an hour, the girls finally left the store. Kara ended up buying two white shirts. One for her, one for Envy, and a pair of capris as well. They caught the J train and headed back to Brooklyn.

"Oh boy, I hate riding on the same car as bums. They stink up the whole train," Kara complained as she nodded toward a bum that was taking up two whole seats.

One seat was him and his beer, the other seat was his bag of what smelled like garbage.

"Me, too, and I can't breathe. I'm trying not to inhale that smell. Let's switch cars," Envy suggested as she and Kara headed toward the sliding door to switch cars.

"Envy, you know that you are scared to switch cars while the train is moving."

"Oh well, I'd rather take my chances than to inhale another minute of that smell."

The girls entered the next car and there was a little Mexican lady selling all types of candy.

"Wait a minute, KARA! I need some candy because my mouth is dry," Envy said and stopped to order a pack of Juicy Fruit from the lady.

"Oh, yea, I want some chocolate," Kara responded before ordering an Almond Joy from the Mexican lady.

Luckily, the girls found a seat together. As they were sitting down, a group of boys with a boom box blasting music entered the car. They stopped the music and demanded everyone's attention.

"Ladies and gentlemen, sorry to interrupt, but we are trying to raise money for college. We are gonna dance for you, and if you can donate, my partner will be collecting change, dollars, or whatever you can spare," a young boy said just before they started the music and begin their performance.

The boys danced for a few minutes to a mix tape as the train moved from one station to the next. I can't front, the boys had talent because they got busy. Envy reached in her pocket to give them some change once they were done.

"No, Envy, we might need that change to get something to eat," Kara stated.

"Don't be like that, Kara. We bless them, you never know how God will bless us," Envy answered.

"You love to give to charity!" Kara said as she rolled her eyes.

"So what! Sharing is caring and they deserve it," Envy immediately responded.

"But Envy, you know those boys are not saving for college. That is the ultimate subway hustle! People dancing and singing for money and acting like it's a donation for a good cause. Come on,

Envy. You should know that by now," Kara reminded Envy of the scam.

"So what! They worked hard for it, and that's what matters," Envy said as she placed the change in the guy's baseball cap. After the guys received all they could get, they moved to the next cart with the same routine.

Once the girls reached Gates Ave, they went to Envy's crib. They were chilling for a minute, then out of nowhere, Envy says, "Kara, I have something to show you."

"What is it, Envy?" Kara curiously asked.

"You know that I couldn't leave them capris, right?" she said as she laughed and pulled down her sweat pants to show off the Versace capris.

"Well, with that being said, I couldn't afford these Iceberg slacks, but I couldn't leave them in the store, either," Kara said as she pulled the slacks from underneath her sweater.

They both laughed and discussed how they couldn't leave the clothes and elaborated on how they took the clothing and how easy it was to take. After a few minutes, Kara finally went home and Envy laid out her clothes for a job appointment. She was excited and by the time she finished, her mother and cousins had already fallen to sleep. Envy crawled into bed with them.

For some reason, Envy loved to sleep with her mother. So she crawled up next to Mercedes, while Earl was in his toddler bed that was placed in Mercedes bedroom and Dre was in between Mercedes and Envy.

Chapter 9

THE NEXT DAY

Envy and India were placed to work at Tompkins Park as daycare teacher assistants. After about two weeks of India being obnoxious, continuously laughing out loud, and slick talking the director, she was sent back to the agency and placed somewhere else. Envy didn't leave with India because she felt that India got herself into that mess, not to mention that she enjoyed her job.

Tompkins Park was convenient for Envy being that it was only two blocks away from her home and right in the hood. "Ocki" (the Arabs) store or Poppy and 'em (the Puerto Ricans) stores are on every corner. You can also find a pizza shop, Mama's Soul Food and a Chinese restaurant mixed up between the corner stores. And even though the 79th Precinct was across the street from the park, it was nothing for gunshots to ring out. Envy also enjoyed watching the fellas walking through the park and playing basketball all day, every day! Girl, bye. India better get over it.

One Friday, there was a concert at Tompkins Park. Immature, the hottest group at the time, was performing. Envy had to help set up and after work, she went to get India to come back to the concert with her.

"India, do you wanna come with me to see Immature at Tompkins Park? I can bring a guest on my V.I.P. pass," Envy explained.

"No, I hate that park. I will never step foot in there again!" India complained, treating Envy with a cold shoulder.

"What's wrong with you?" Envy asked, feeling the tension from India.

"Nothing is wrong with me. I just don't understand how you could betray our friendship like that. If I had to leave, you should have left, too," India sarcastically questioned their friendship.

Envy sucked her teeth before responding, "It is what it is, India! I'm not about to kiss your butt because you got fired. I didn't do it to you, you did this to yourself!" Envy shot back being just a sassy as India. "If you weren't so loud, you would still be there. I'm not mad and I'm not entertaining your attitude. I'm out," Envy stated as she walked away from India toward the door.

"Fine then! I DON'T CARE, EITHER!" India yelled while slamming and locking the door behind Envy.

Envy went to Kara's house and she was down to go. Kara was in love with Batman and Envy loved Romeo. Everybody and their momma was going to be out there. LITERALLY! They agreed to meet up just before the show. Both of them had to be decked out for the concert.

Envy went home, jumped in the shower and did her usual three washes and cold water rinses. Afterward, she brushed her teeth and dipped a lil' Versace Red Jeans perfume all over her body on top of the vanilla sugar body lotion to add an extra tantalizing scent. She took her time combing down her wrap and fixing her face, nothing superficial because she wasn't into makeup. Envy was making sure everything, including her eyebrows and lips were on point as usual before getting dressed.

Envy couldn't wait to slip on her brand-new black Versace capris. They went perfectly with a black and white DKNY fitted shirt she had in the closet. It was something casual. The outfit complemented her black ankle length boots, yea, the ones that India loved, and, of course, she had to dip into her mother's jewelry box for the finishing touches.

After double checking herself in their diamond shaped mirrors on the wall that showed the full body, Envy was looking just right! She was ready to go. Thank God Mercedes and the boys were not home because she had a chance to escape without being questioned.

When she reached Kara's crib, Kara was already dressed. Envy was the only slow poke, just like her mother.

"Kara, you look nice!" Envy complimented while checking out her friend's outfit.

"You do, too! Aww, look at you! Why are you dressed so sexy? You make me wanna change. I look like a little girl," Kara responded with a compliment of her own, feeling a little underdressed compared to Envy.

Kara was dressed in a cute powder blue and gray Iceberg jogging short set with her blue ankle pom-pom socks and some beautiful looking powder blue and gray Air Max 95s. Kara loved to wear loose fitting jogging suits because she liked for her booty to jiggle. She was slim but thick with it. Her hair was in a wrap but she had it pinned up on each side and let the back hang. Kara had a good grade of hair that draped just past her shoulders.

"Oh please, Kara! You look nice, too, and you are fresh as hell. I never saw this outfit before. I didn't know that you had it," Envy said, feeling on the material. "And your Air Max are fresh! What's the problem? I don't see what's wrong with you."

"But look at you Envy. You look at least 17 or 18. I look every bit of 14," Kara joked before giggling.

"Listen, Kara, this is just my style, and that's your style. We both look good rockin' our own style. Now come on, girl."

"I'm just saying. I wish I would've known that you were going to look this sexy. I would've at least thrown on my pink and white Baby Phat dress," Kara responded before the girls got ready to leave.

As they walked toward the door, Envy noticed the last piece that was missing from her outfit. "OOO, whose purse is this!?" Envy questioned after spotting a pretty black and white purse with the gold Versace head as the buckle.

"It's mine, why? You wanna use it?" Kara asked.

"Yes, now tell me this is not a perfect match with my outfit," Envy stated as she modeled the purse with her outfit.

"Yes, it is but now I don't have a pocketbook," Kara agreed before laughing.

Envy ignored Kara's comment and continued to put her things in the purse on their way out of the door. Envy thought to herself, *Damn why she keeps comparing herself to me in every way? It seems like she wants to be me. But I'm going to overlook it because she's my friend.*

The girls went to the concert and it was OFF THE HOOK! As they walked through the crowded park in their cute outfits, of course, the fellas were gazing and hollering at them. Kara's Uncle Bezo was there and Envy's brother Jah and his crew were in the crowd somewhere so that was out. The haters hated and the frenemies spoke and whispered while the associates acknowledged them and vice versa.

They made their way to the V.I.P section, sat down and enjoyed the show. Some of the local dance groups, rap groups, and R&B groups performed before Immature. And once they stepped on the stage, the girls went bananas! Chicks were trying to jump on the stage and all.

Being that Envy worked there, after the concert, she and Kara were able to chill with the group backstage. They had fun being in the presence of Immature. The group gave the girls their own special performance as they sang, “I will never lie again...you will always be my friend…” Envy and Kara were in a zone. They didn’t hear a word that came out of the boys’ mouths. Envy fantasized about losing her virginity that night as she gazed at Romeo's lips and looked in his eyes. Oh, it was overwhelming and a dream come true!

Moments before the park cleared, Envy and Kara decided to walk to the store. As soon as they reached the gate to leave the park, things got crazy.

POW! POW! POW! POW! POW! POW! POW!

Gunshots filled the air! The girls ducked and ran back toward the crowd only to find out that they were running in the direction of the shots. The girls then ran back the other way, toward their homes and didn’t stop until they had reached Quincy and Throop, which was a block away from the park. Envy’s wonderful brother was okay and as the girls caught their breaths, they spotted Shane.

“Hey, Shane, where is my brother? Is he okay?”

"Yeah, he left about 30 minutes ago with this little red bone shorty."

"What about Corey?" Envy continued.

"He's good. He didn't even come to the park. But look, I gotta go. You girls be careful," Shane stated before walking off and the girls went their way.

Envy was relieved to know that her brother and Corey were okay. Jah had been getting a little wild since Ty was murdered. As they walked down Throop trying to shake off the excitement of the night, who did they see?

"Envy, when did India start hanging out with Vikki?" Kara asked after spotting the two of them across the street talking to one another.

Envy looked across the street and yep, it was true. India was with Vikki from school. "That fat trick is fake! I'm not messing with her anymore. Forget her! She mad because she got fired and I didn't quit my assignment with her. Whatever!" Envy sarcastically stated as she rolled her eyes, dismissing what she was seeing.

As they reached the block, everybody and their momma were out talking about the concert.

Kara stopped to talk to her friend from 671, another building on their block. Envy spoke but she really didn't deal with the chicks on Gates Ave other than Kara and India, no offense. But it is what it is, so Envy kept it moving.

"Kara, I'll holla at you later," Envy spoke softly before going upstairs.

Mercedes was on the phone with Jessica when Envy entered the house. She couldn't help but hear her mother mentioning that Jah had gotten arrested. Hearing the news bothered Envy because she thought he was chilling with a shorty.

After Mercedes got off of the phone, she explained to Envy that Jah was locked up. He'd gotten caught with a gun and drugs on him. He was going to be spending the weekend in jail before seeing the judge and getting a bail.

Envy politely excused herself from the conversation because she was upset. She went into her bedroom to cry. One, Jah was her only brother and she hated to hear any bad news involving him because that was her heart. It was like when Jah was in trouble she could feel his pain. Even when Mercedes whipped them. Envy cried harder for Jah than she would cry for herself. And two, Jah promised to give her some money when he returned home that evening.

After about an hour of crying, Envy fell asleep. Mercedes know that there was a special love that Envy and Jah shared. She decided to leave Envy alone because she saw Envy's eyes getting watery during the conversation.

Later that evening, Mercedes checked on Envy and noticed that she fell asleep in her clothes, shoes, and all. If Envy went to bed without wrapping her hair, something was terribly wrong! She turned Envy's light and TV off and went to her room to pray for her son. After 30 minutes of praise and worship, Mercedes went to bed herself, worrying about what was going on with her only son as he spiraled out of control.

Chapter 10

THE HATE IS REAL

The next day, Mercedes needed some time to herself so Earl and Dre went to Jessica's house and allowed Envy to be monitored by Stacey. By the time Envy reached Putnam Ave, Nay and Taya were on their way to Marcy pool. Envy met them in front of 300, which was their building number (300 Putnam Avenue).

"Did you bring your bathing suit, Blillz?" Nay asked Envy.

"Yea, I got it on under my dress," Envy responded.

"Envy, is that the dress that you're wearing all day? Taya asked.

"No, I'm going back home to get dressed after we leave the pool," Envy answered.

"I thought your mother was going out to relieve some stress. And what happened with your brother?" Nay questioned.

"My mother left already. And I won't know what's going on with my brother until Monday," Envy answered quickly and nonchalantly, not wanting to get into a conversation about Jah's business.

First of all, it was a touchy subject and secondly, Mercedes raised them to never tell what went on at home. If she wanted anyone to know, she would tell it.

"So Nay, what's up with you and Mario? Are yal kickin' it for real or what?" Envy asked, quickly changing the subject and Nay smiled.

"I like him a lot. He comes over every day with his brother Champ. Me and Taya be in the hallway with them," Nay responded.

"What yal be doing?" Envy blurted out before giggling.

"Ughhh, nothing!" Nay answered.

"Yes, they do! Nay, stop lying. Yal be kissing," Taya interjected.

"Mind your business, Taya, and worry about you and Champ!" Nay fired back.

"I don't really like Champ. Plus, he's always asking for Envy," Taya responded, going back and forth with Nay.

"ME!?" Envy shouted in a surprised tone.

"Yea, he like you, Envy. I didn't tell you because I thought Taya liked him," Nay stated.

"Well, I like Steven anyway." Taya responded.

"Envy, are you going to talk to Champ?" Nay asked.

"I don't know. He is cute," Envy stated.

"Tell me so that I can hook it up. And Mario keeps asking me to go out with him. I told him that I will give him an answer later. Envy, what do you think that I should do?" Nay asked.

"Well, do what you want if you like him. Why not go out with him? And after the pool, I'll give you an answer about Champ," Envy replied as the girls continued walking to the pool.

They finally reach Marcy pool and once they entered the gate, immediately noticed that it was crowded. The whole hood was there for the 2nd session.

"What up, yal?" Aubrey spoke to Nay and Taya.

She and Envy looked at each other and simultaneously rolled their eyes. Envy couldn't stand her. She was the type that was loud for no reason. Every time Envy would visit Nay and 'em, Aubrey would come in the hallway with her Aunt Mia and cousin Aretha. She would be so loud and evil just because.

"Meanwhile, back at the ranch…"

They went through the gate and it was on and poppin'! It just so happened that Mario and Champ were already there. Envy and Nay really had to show off.

"Envy, you just want to drop your towel and switch past the boys so they can look at your butt," Nay stated as Envy began to unwrap her towel from around her waist.

“So what, Nay! I got it, so if that’s what I wanna do, why not? I got it and the fellas are here, why not show off a lil’ bit?” Envy boasted as she smirked even though that was not her intentions.

Now Nay was the type that liked to get in front of a crowd of boys and call you out. She always did that to Envy. But Envy didn’t mind because Nay would feel stupid because her actions didn’t faze Envy. Envy would do the opposite of what Nay expected. Nay intended to embarrass Envy but she wouldn’t feed into it and act as if that’s exactly what she wanted to do.

Nay didn’t know that she was only drawing attention to Envy every time she tried to stunt in front of a dude, and Envy loved attention. So, at the end of the day, Nay would end up mad.

Envy threw her towel off and switched past the group of guys, then past another group, as they all stopped and stared. Envy purposely kneeled down slowly to put her feet in the water. As soon as Envy was close enough to the water, that hatin' chick Aubrey pushed Envy in the pool.

At first, Envy thought it was Nay because she was known for doing stupid stuff like that but when she turned, noticed Nay laughing her hardest, while Aubrey ran past pointing and laughing. Envy jumped out of the pool to chase her, which was right up her alley because all of the dudes were watching. It was Aubrey's lucky day because the life guard blew the whistle for them to stop running because Envy wanted some payback. Instead, Envy just got back into the water with Taya.

"She only did that because the boys were staring and Nay is only laughing that hard because Mario was looking too." Taya stated while enjoying the cool pool.

"I know but I don't even play with her like that, watch when I catch her." Envy stated.

"And Nay why would you be sitting there laughing that hard at someone trying to humiliate your family?" Taya questioned.

"What? Does Aubrey think she made herself like I was look good?" Envy asked Nay as she walked to the edge of the pool.

"What do you mean? UGGGH! She was just playing with you. You always gotta get personal," Nay responded with an attitude.

"How would you feel if I did that to you? But I'm not mad. it's cool," Envy brushed it off while playing in the water.

“Ha-ha-ha! That was funny. That was a good one…” Aubrey went on to rub it in.

“It wasn’t that funny. Alright, it’s OVER!” Envy spoke in an agitated tone.

“Don’t nobody tell me when I can laugh. I can laugh at what I want. Ha, ha, ha…” Aubrey sarcastically responded before she burst out laughing again.

“Yo, I’m about to break out because I don’t want to ruin anyone’s day. I’m out!” Envy stated as she got out of the pool and headed directly towards the locker room.

“That’s why I hate taking her places, because she always does that,” Nay complained.

“Nay, don’t do that because that’s our cousin, and Aubrey shouldn’t have pushed her,” Taya defended Envy before getting out of the pool.

“Alright, Taya, but she knew it was just a joke. She didn’t have to get all serious and stuff,” Nay snapped back.

“But how would you feel if everybody was sitting around, laughing and clowning on you?” Taya barked back.

"I don't like her anyway, so even if it wasn't funny. I still was going to laugh my hardest," Aubrey continued with the smart remarks.

"Don't be laughing at my cousin because she doesn't like you, either!" Taya swiftly replied before walking toward the locker room.

"I will laugh at you!" Aubrey boldly said.

"No… laugh at getting your teeth fixed," Taya spat back as she left.

Envy was walking and thinking, *I shouldn't leave. I'm giving Aubrey what she wants. She wants all of the attention, but with my body being more developed than hers, that takes the focus off of her. She would rather me off the scene.*

Taya interrupted her thoughts, "WAIT FOR ME, ENVY. I'm leaving with you. Nay's two faced self get on my nerves!"

"What happened?" Envy stops and asks.

"No, because she sitting there clowning and laughing just because Aubrey is laughing at you. Like I told her, you are our cousin and she shouldn't do that!" Taya stated as they entered the locker room to change their clothes before leaving.

"It's cool, Taya! I'm not mad at all. One thing Jah always told me 'if you can't take the heat, get off of the playing field.' And I'm out before I punch that raggedy mouth chick Aubrey in her face. I'd rather just leave."

Envy walked Taya back to Putnam then she headed home. After getting home, Envy wasted no time fixing her something to eat and getting dressed. While she was getting dressed, Envy received a call from Izel. They made plans to walk through Malcolm X Boulevard to check out David and his crew. So yes, Envy had to put on her finest. She kept it simple but cute.

She threw on her lime green and gray Guess sweater dress with her matching lime green 54/11s. She then brushed her hair back into a ponytail because she had enough hair to make one and threw on her jewelry before patiently waiting for Izel.

RING! RING! RING!

"Hello," Envy answered.

"YO, ENVY, COME OVER HERE! ME AND AUBREY JUST GOT INTO A FIGHT! I JUST BEAT HER UP FOR TALKING TRASH ABOUT YOU. NOW SHE'S WAITING TO FIGHT YOU!" Taya yelled loudly as she could into the phone.

Envy had never heard Taya speak in that tone so she knew that it was serious. "SHE WHAT!? You what? Oh, yal fought? You should've called me first but I'm on my way," Envy responded shocked at Taya's comment.

Before she could hang up, a male voice Envy immediately recognized as Uncle Marvin's yelled in the background, "NO, ENVY! DON'T COME OVER HERE! TAYA ALREADY BEAT HER DOWN. YOU STAY HOME!"

"BUT UNCLE MARVIN, SHE WANTS TO FIGHT! SHE KEEPS STARTING!" Envy yelled back, anxious to fight.

"IF SHE REALLY WANTED TO FIGHT YOU, LIKE TAYA TOLD HER, YOU JUST LEFT. SHE WOULD'VE POPPED OFF THEN INSTEAD OF TALKING BEHIND YOUR BACK. DON'T WORRY. TAYA WAXED THAT BUTT. SHE DOESN'T WANT NO MORE. TRUST ME!"

"Okay, Uncle. I'm not going to come but tell Taya to call me back later."

Ding dong!

The doorbell rang.

“Alright, Uncle Marvin.” Envy replied before hanging up the phone and going to see who was at the door. “WHO IS IT!?” Envy screamed just before she looked through the peephole.

“It’s me, Izel.”

Envy opened the door. “What’s good, son? Who buzzed you in downstairs?”

“That chick Dee Dee and her homegirls were coming out of the building as I was coming in. I hope you ready because you always taking mad long,” Izel commented while standing in the doorway.

“I’m ready. Let’s go.”

As the girls walked to Malcolm X, Envy schooled Izel on what took place at Marcy pool and the fight between Taya and Aubrey.

“Damn, son, Nay shouldn’t have done that. She better be lucky that wrap didn’t get messy. Then it would’ve been problems,” Izel stated as she nodded toward Envy’s hair.

“Her little self didn't even push me hard, that’s why I wasn’t mad. It’s just the aftermath that made it worse. Then she played it like oh well. But I understood her actions,” Envy smirked. “I’m not mad, though. However, when I catch Aubrey, that's another story," Envy continued.

The girls decided to hang out on Hancock and Malcolm X because the Hancock and Stuyvesant corner were whack as usual. The Malcolm X end was always poppin'. It didn't take long before Envy and David noticed each other and they walked toward each other's direction. As they hugged and greeted one another, Izel was talking to her honey.

"Izel, come here. Let me holla at you," Envy said. "Look, I'm staying the night with David. But I'll walk you back when you're ready."

"Okay, son. That's cool. Ima chill over here for a while. Don't nobody wanna be near my mother when she's drunk," Izel replied.

"Okay, that's cool."

As the group chilled, Izel and some of the dude's smoked, while, for some reason, Envy and David were so into each other. After a couple of hours, Izel was ready to leave. David was nice enough to put her in a cab. Envy stayed with David and then left bright and early the next morning.

Envy ran into India's cousin Torrey, who had been staying with India for a while.

"What's up, Envy? Where you going?"

"Nowhere but upstairs, that's about it," Envy reluctantly answered.

"Oh, I'm walking to Putnam later to see my friend Tia. Can you walk me over there?" Torrey asked.

"What time is later? And Putnam and what?" Envy asked with her eyebrows raised at the sound of Putman.

"Later on when the sun goes down. And Putnam and Marcy. India has been with her newfound friend Vikki for the past couple of days so it's hard to get her to do anything," Torrey stated.

"Yea, I know but I'll walk with you. Just ring my bell when you're ready," Envy responded before going upstairs.

She showered, lounged around the house, and reminisced about her time with David. No, they didn't have sex!! Everything was just right; except for his mother. David introduced Envy to his mother Miss Tricia for the 5th time, but she was such a witch that you crumbled in her presence. Her face looked hard and she even talked hard. Envy fell asleep daydreaming about David. She was in such a deep sleep that she didn't even answer the phone! That was unusual.

When Envy finally woke up, she threw on some clothes. What Torrey had asked was right up her alley. Putnam Avenue! She had to call first to make sure Stacey and Uncle Marvin weren't home being that they told her not to come over there to fight.

Envy called three times but got no answer. That was enough verification for her. They had mentioned that Envy's grandparents from her father's side were having a cookout but Envy really didn't deal with them too much, so she wasn't pressed to go with them. Later on that night, Torrey rang the bell and she and Envy went to Putnam as planned.

It looked like a setup but it wasn't because Torrey didn't know what was going on. Her homegirl living on that block was just a coincidence. Once they reached Putnam Ave, Aubrey and her crew were outside as usual. That's when Envy schooled Torrey on what was about to take place.

"Don't worry, Envy. I got your back. As long as nobody jump in, we're good."

After about 20 minutes of sitting on Torrey's homegirl's stoop, Envy decided to press Aubrey. As soon as she started loud talking, Envy busted her dead in her grill. That stupid broad couldn't fight. She was nothing but mouth. Envy wore her out so bad that her big, fat, 300-pound Aunt Mia had to jump in but she didn't do much. She was too fat to move. Envy had some hair out of place and a broken nail but was able to handle them both for a moment.

Envy got it poppin'! Mario and 'em recorded the fight; that's how crucial it was. After 3 rounds of getting her butt whipped, Aubrey decided that she didn't wanna fight anymore. Envy chased her upstairs. A few minutes later, Aubrey returned with a baseball bat! When she came back downstairs with the bat, Envy was reluctant to fight her with it.

"PUT THE BAT DOWN! YOU BAD!" Envy taunted Aubrey as she kept her distance.

"NO! I'M ABOUT TO BEAT THE BLACK OFF OF YOU WITH IT!" Aubrey yelled back while standing her ground.

They went back and forth for a while but Aubrey never swung the bat. Envy noticed that Aubrey really didn't have the heart. Instead, she was soft as butter. Envy walked away and Aubrey followed behind her talking trash, but still never swung her bat.

"Envy, stop walking. Don't run. Fight her!" Torrey instigated, although she hadn't helped Envy at all.

"What do I look like? Why would I run up on a bat?" Envy asked as she looked at Torrey as if she was crazy. Envy thought, *You let me get jumped. What in the hell are you going to do if I get beat with a bat?* Envy was no joke so after a few minutes of thinking about it, she said, "Later for that. You're right!"

Envy stopped walking and turned around, picked up a bottle and cracked it on the ground before yelling, "I DARE YOU TO HIT ME WITH THAT BAT!"

"OH, NOW YOU WANNA CUT ME!?" Aubrey asked.

"NO TIME FOR QUESTIONS! SWING THAT BAT, THAT'S ALL I'M SAYING!" Envy spoke boldly while walking towards Aubrey and playing her bluff.

Aubrey never swung her bat, no matter how many people told her to hit Envy with the bat and no matter how many times Envy dared her. She just wanted to cause a scene so Envy and 'em left.

On the way home, Envy was quiet. In her mind, that was her last time chilling with Torrey because when things hit the fan, Torrey was not a rider. She didn't even try to break it up while Envy was getting jumped. Envy saw her standing way back in the street. India always made her family more than who they were, and Torrey was not that gorilla unit chick that India made her out to be. She turned out to be a fraud just like India!

Once they reached Gates Ave, Envy walked straight to her building like it was nothing. "Alright, Torrey, Ima holla at you."

"Alright, Envy, Ima' ring your bell tomorrow."

"Yea, aiight," Envy stated nonchalantly as they departed, knowing that she was done with Torrey.

Envy was the type of person that you wouldn't know if she's mad at you or the situation. She wouldn't say anything. She'd just stop rocking with you.

* * * * *

The royal rumble

The next day, Envy told her family what happened the night before. Mercedes hadn't returned from her secret rendezvous. Stacey told Envy to come back over there on that Sunday afternoon and she and Aubrey would shoot the fair one.

Once Envy reached Putnam, the whole Marcy PJs was there. That's how Envy's family rolled. They get it poppin'! And once Envy arrived, it was on. Envy ran up on Aubrey even though she still had her bat. Uncle Marvin snatched the bat out of her hand and it was a wrap.

It was a royal rumble out there. Marcy Projects against Putnam Ave. Really, it was Marcy against Aubrey and her family, because the others were out there watching. Things really got hectic when Mia ran up behind Stacey and hit her in the back of the head with a bat. Stacy hit the ground and laid there for a moment and all hell broke loose on Mia. Envy's peeps lit her up like a Christmas tree and Aubrey ran!

After what seem to be an hour of fighting, Envy and her family went upstairs to Stacey's apartment. After about 10 minutes, the doorbell rang.

DING DONG! DING DONG!

"WHO IS IT?" Uncle Marvin yelled from the living room as he put ice on a huge knot on the back of Stacey's head.

"IT'S THE POLICE!"

Everyone got quiet. "Yal chill, it's the police!" Stacey whispered before opening the door while holding a small towel filled with ice to the back of her head.

They asked for Envy's family side of the story and still ended up locking Stacey and her sister Neila up. The police had to lock them up because Aubrey and her family were beaten pretty bad. Uncle Marvin took Envy to the police station to tell her side of the story.

After hearing Envy's side of the story and finding out that Aubrey had instigated the fight, the police released Stacey and 'em. Not to mention that Mia, Aubrey or any of their family's stories added up.

After that day, the drama was over. Envy never had another problem with Aubrey. All of that loudness and rudeness when she was in Envy's presence was over. Aubrey barely looked Envy's way when they crossed paths.

See, you never know how real a person is until they are put to the test. The people that talk a lot and are loud are usually not a threat. They make noise but the one that's quiet are true threats. You will never see or expect it coming. A demonstration is better than a conversation!

Chapter 11

ALBANY DAY

That Monday, Mercedes bailed out Jah and couldn't understand why he was choosing to live the life of the streets. Both Mercedes and Envy did their best to talk some sense into him but he wasn't trying to hear it. Since he was much older than Envy, Mercedes was done trying to punish him for the things he got himself into and it was the last time she would bail him out.

After the fight on Putnam, Envy, on the other hand, was put on punishment for a whole month for being disobedient. Mercedes felt if Uncle Marvin told Envy not to come around to avoid the fight, then that's what Envy should have done. Stacey being hit with a bat and the police being on the scene was enough for Mercedes and Envy was to blame.

As for Envy, she learned her lesson and was in desperate need to see outside again. It was early August and she thought that her summer would be over. Other than work, doing laundry, going to the store, and going to church, outside was a mystery to Envy.

Mercedes later changed her punishment to two weeks and after a long two weeks, Envy had her freedom back and she was glad the day had come! The good thing about this day was that it was a Saturday and it was Albany Day!

Albany Day is when they block all cars from entering the project parking lot and bring out the DJ equipment. The DJ played all of the latest hits in hip hop, R&B, and reggae, not to mention the people performing to a little calypso. All types of fun activities are going on.

"Ma, don't I get off punishment today?" Envy anxiously asked.

"I'm not sure. I think it's tomorrow," Mercedes answered in a sarcastic tone, knowing that she was picking with Envy.

"No ma'am, no, no… I have been on a countdown. Today is my day. See, look. You said I can get off the Saturday before the actual two weeks if I behave. You made me mark the calendar, and I put a line through each day of my punishment. And today is my last day because I haven't given you any trouble," Envy pleaded her case as she jumped around and clapped her hands. "Can I go to Albany Day?" Envy excitedly asked.

"Ah, I don't think so. I'm sick and tired of everywhere that you go, you get into a fight!" Mercedes stated.

"But Ma, I learned my lesson. Please, Ma… pleeeease, I promise not to get into anything, just trust me this one last time."

"Every time I trust you to do the right thing, you always fail. So why should I trust you now?" Mercedes ask.

"Because I really learned my lesson this time. The other times I was being stupid, but being on punishment for so long, not being able to hang out with my friends was miserable for me," Envy answered.

"And just who supposed to be going with you to this Albany Day?" Mercedes ask.

"Me and Dora but you know Lulu and 'em will be there to watch us," Envy continued pleading her case.

"I'm going to let you go this time and you better not let me down, or should I say, let yourself down. Because if you do, this time, your punishment will be for 1 year!" Mercedes threatened.

"Thanks, Ma. And one more thing. I need an outfit and a pair of sneakers because I don't have nothing to wear."

"Now you're getting carried away! Outfit and sneakers? You are not being rewarded," Mercedes quickly denied.

"Well, I got paid today. I can reward myself. Plus, I still have my other check that I was not allowed to cash while I was on punishment," Envy stated as she waved her check back and forth.

"Yea, whatever," Mercedes responded, staring reluctantly at Envy before saying, "Well, as long as you have your own money go ahead and you better be home by 9:30, and I mean it!"

Envy headed to downtown Brooklyn. Usually she would hit up Century 21, but she didn't have time to go to Manhattan, so instead she stayed local. She wanted to use her time wisely. As she stood in front her building waiting on the B 52, this dude pulled up in a money green Lexus coupe and rolled his passenger window down.

"Hey, Ma, what's up?" dude hollered and Envy ignored him. He then stepped out the "V" (vehicle) and as he approached, he said, "Hey, Ma, what's up with you?" He held out his hand to greet Envy.

"Hiii," Envy softly responded as she blushed. She was so shy.

"So what's your name?"

"My name is Envy, what's yours?"

"I'm Glen but they call me Money," he responded as he winked at her.

She smiled as she shied away from him. It's something about Glen that caught Envy's eye. He was a handsome brown skinned fella with big, bright eyes and his facial hair cut neatly into a goatee. He was exactly her height with long braids and a charming personality. Envy could tell by the Versace outfit and wheels how he earned the name Money.

"So where you headed?" Glen asked.

"Downtown," she answered.

"I'm headed that way, too. Hop in. I can give you a ride," he suggested but Envy declined.

"Nah, I'm good. Ima take the bus," Envy stated.

“Nah, Ma. You don’t have to catch the bus. I’m more than happy to take you,” Glen answered.

Envy declined again, knowing that she wanted to hop in that coupe, but instead, she chose to play the ‘I don’t need your ride, I’m good’ role. She knew that in the long run, it would make him sweat her harder because she didn’t hop in his whip.

“I see you a tuff lil momma. Here, take my pager number anyway and hit me when you have time,” he smoothly spoke, full of confidence.

Thank God Envy was stunting with Mercedes’ cell phone. Envy got his number and shortly after he drove off, her bus came. The bus was soooo crowded. There were no seats and barely anywhere to stand. It was so noisy on the bus and this baby had the nerve to start screaming and hollering. Envy couldn’t wait to hit downtown Brooklyn. She was so anxious that she got off at the beginning of downtown’s shopping strip instead of waiting for it to hit Hoyt Street which would’ve put her directly in the midst of the shopping area.

Once Envy reached downtown, she glanced in several stores but nothing really caught her eye.

See, this is why I go to Centuries, Envy thought to herself. Century 21 was more diverse and very few people from Brooklyn shopped there. They had any and everything that Envy wanted and she would not have to worry about seeing somebody rocking the same outfit.

Envy was getting agitated as she sucked her teeth in disgust because she'd been in over a half a dozen stores and had not found anything to wear. It was 3 o'clock when she began to think about how much time she would have to hang out before her 9:30 curfew.

"This is my last store. If I can't find nothing, then I'm not going!" Envy spoke out loud to no one as she walked into Ladies' Dr. Jays.

She wasn't in there more than five minutes when something caught her eye. Envy was drawn to these yellow and black Mountain Gear boots and she couldn't help but try them on. They looked cute on her feet as she imagined how they would look with a little mini skirt.

"How much are these?" Envy spoke softly to a sales clerk that was walking by.

"$65 plus tax," the sales clerk stopped and answered.

"Okay, I want these. Do yal have any jean skirts?"

"Follow me, I'll show you what we have," the sales clerk instructed with a smile.

Envy spotted a dark jean Calvin Klein mini skirt. She priced it and Bam! It was on sale for $15. Now all she needed was a shirt. Envy walked around for a few as the clerk helped another customer and noticed an orange and yellow tank top that went perfectly with the boots and the skirt. The yellow in the tank top picked up the yellow stitching in the boot, and the orange lining picked up the orange stitching in the skirt. It was a perfect outfit!

"Excuse me. Where is your fitting room?" Envy wanted to know.

"Follow me right this way," the clerk responded and Envy followed her to the back of the store.

She entered the fitting room. "Oh yes, this matches perfectly!" Envy spoke out loud while admiring the outfit with the boots on. *Perfect,* she thought as she undressed and exited the fitting room, pleased with her choice. She approached the register and handed over what she didn't want before paying for her outfit and boots. Envy had everything she needed and quickly hurried home to change.

Once Envy entered her apartment, it was empty. She was thrilled because now she could get dressed and leave without the extra stuff that Mercedes would have to put her through. Envy quickly bumped and wrapped her hair, jumped in the shower and got dressed. She pranced around in front of the mirror as usual, making sure everything was on point before heading to Albany. Thank God she had money left for a cab because it was getting late.

It was a couple minutes after five when Envy got out of the cab on St Marks near Albany Projects and the corner was poppin'! I mean, everybody that was somebody was out there. Envy was 14 but she always had an eye for the older guys. Too bad they were her cousin's friends or her brother, Jah's peeps. Luckily, Envy ran into Dora by the store so she didn't have to walk through the crowd alone.

"What's up, cuz? When you got over here?" Dora blurted out with her loud voice.

"I just got out a cab," Envy answered.

"Oh, come on. We about to walk back to the projects," Dora stated as she pointed at close to a dozen other chicks.

There was one thing Envy couldn't stand and that was to be with a flock of chicks, especially loud ones. Envy was from the hood, but there was nothing hood about her except for she didn't take no mess at all.

“Yo’ D, come on, son. They ‘bout to dance,” one of the chicks by the name of Missy blurted out.

The group of them walked through the projects laughing and chatting with others until they reached the circle where the performances took place. Envy enjoyed about 5 to 6 dance groups, a couple of rap groups and a few singers. The last one to perform was Little Vicious and the crowd went wild when he performed his latest hit, “Freaks.”

Envy, Dora, and the crew danced and sang to the Jamaican song. Dora and her crew were smoking their weed and drinking their liquor, something that Envy was not into. The last day of school was her first and last time smoking. And drinking wasn’t her thing so she flew off of her natural high.

The mood was right, then came Dolla, a light skinned honey with big, brown eyes and dreadlocks that every chick in and outside of the projects had a crush on. Dolla was a great dancer, especially to reggae music. As he danced, Envy watched through her peripheral vision and couldn’t help but to cut her eye from time to time.

“Why you looking at my son like that?” a deep voice whispered in Envy’s ear and when she turned to look, notice that it was Ray, Dolla’s father. He and his son looked just alike except Ray had some pretty salt-and-pepper hair that he kept wavy.

She smiled and answered, “I’m just watching everybody.”

“Nah, you looking at him like you want something,” Ray joked around.

“No, it’s not like that,” she responded before bashfully laughing.

“It better not be. If so, don’t be scared. YO, DOLLA, COME HERE!” Ray spoke loudly over the music, waving his hand for his son to come where they were standing.

“What up, Pops? Dolla asked as he walked toward them, wiping the sweat off of his head.

“She’s checking you out. Isn’t this Dora’s cousin?” Ray asks.

“Yea, that’s Dora cousin. What is she looking at, with her chocolate self?” Dolla curiously asked, blushing at Envy.

“That’s what I just asked her, but she seems a little scared.” Ray had Envy on the spot.

“Scared of what? I was just watching everybody dancing. I don’t know what you’re talking about,” Envy came back in her own defense.

“She scared, Pops? Ima leave her alone until she’s ready,” Dolla stated before dancing his way back into the crowd.

Envy continued to mingle with who she was familiar with, whine to a couple of reggae songs, jumped to a couple of calypso hits and sang a couple of rap lyrics. The final performance was a local artist by the name of Half a Mil from Albany Projects and his music was poppin’! He did his thing and had the crowd rocking and before Envy knew it, it was 8:30.

“Alright, Dora, I gotta go.”

“Wait, Envy, don’t leave yet. Why you leaving so soon?” Dora questioned after looking at her watch.

“My mother said that I have to be in by 9, and it’s almost 9 now.”

“Alright, cuz, because we don’t want Mercedes coming over here and showing out. So go ahead. Ima call you tomorrow,” Dora said while giving Envy a hug.

“Alright, Dora,” Envy stated as she walked away.

Somebody grabbed her by the arm and asked, "Where you going, Chocolate?"

Envy looked and noticed that it was Dolla. "I'm going home."

"See you later, but you need to stop being scared of me," Dolla said.

"Whatever!" Envy stated as she turned and spotted her brother stepping quickly to them with fire in his eyes.

"Get your hands off my sister," Jah stated as he grabbed Dolla by the back of his neck

"Yo, what's the problem?" Dolla responded before shaking loose.

Envy quickly jumped in between the two. "Jah, chill! I'm going home, anyway.

"You need some money for a cab?" Jah asked after turning his back to Dolla but she quickly declined.

Dolla walked away as Envy calmed her brother down. While they were talking, a cab pulled up and her brother's friend Shane was in the back. Jah jumped in the cab with him as Envy gathered her thoughts before leaving.

It was five minutes after nine and Envy knew she only had 25 minutes to make it home. She began walking swiftly toward the parking lot to exit the projects.

BOOM! BOOM! BOOM...POW, POW, POW.

Envy ducked down and stood still as the gunshots continued.

POW! POW! POW...

"AHHHHHHHHH!" a voice close by Envy screamed out in pain only moments after her brother had left.

"ENVY, STAY DOWN! DON'T MOVE!" a female voice yelled from behind a parked car.

As Envy turned to see who was talking to her, she immediately noticed her cousin Tami crawling on her knees as the gunfire continued.

POW! POW! POW! BOOM! BOOM!

The sound of different guns being fired continued for a moment until everyone heard the loud sound of a car skidding off.

All hell broke loose when someone screamed, "DADDY! DADDY!"

"I'm, I'm, I'm goo…" Ray coughed before struggling to utter, "I'm good, son."

Envy ran toward the crowd that was gathering around someone on the ground and immediately noticed Ray in a pool of blood fighting for his life. Everyone was screaming and Dolla was hysterical. "NOOOO!" he yelled while down on his knees trying to comfort his father.

"WHAT HAPPENED?" Suzie yelled while hugging Dolla.

"I don't know who it was, Ma," Dolla blurted out as tears flooded his face. "They came to shoot him, Ma, Daddy tried to run with us but one of the guys ran up on him, Ma! Ma, he tried!"

"Noooo! Who were they, Karon?" Suzie asked, calling Dolla by his government name.

"I don't know, Ma!" he continued to repeat as a dark cloud of sadness covered the area.

They tried to keep Ray talking to them until the ambulance pulled up. Ray was slipping in and out of consciousness when the ambulance arrived and immediately began to work on him. They did their best to stop the bleeding before loading him into the ambulance. Suzie rode in the ambulance with Ray and Dolla and the rest of them met up at St. John's Hospital.

"Tami, where did you come from?" Envy asked, still shaking from the event.

"I was walking through the projects and I saw you and your brother so I began to walk over to where yal was posted. Then, all of a sudden, I heard gunshots. I was like, 'No, I got to make it to my little cousins,'" Tami explained while using her hands to animate how she was running.

"I was so glad to see you. It was like you saved my life, for real," Envy nervously spoke.

"Oh my God, yal okay? And Tami, where did you come from?" Dora asked as she walked up on the two of them.

"I was on the old side, walking through here and I heard gun shots, then saw Envy," Tami stated.

“Why they shoot Ray like that? I wonder if he’s alright,” Dora stated while looking around, checking to make sure it was over.

“I’m going home. Dora, call me and tell me what happened,” Envy chimed out loud before walking away.

“Envy, wait, I’m walking that way. Are you getting on the bus or taking a cab?” Tami asked.

“I’m taking a cab. I’m too scared to walk to the bus stop. That incident got me shook.”

Tami and Envy walked to the corner of St Marks, Envy got a cab and Tami went home. Tami also lived in the same building, 959 St Marks, as Dora and their other aunt, Tiny. Tami lived with her mother Gloria, two brothers, Don and Nick, and her sister Meka.

By the time Envy reached Gates Ave, her feet were sore from the Mountain Gears and she was still a little rattled from the gunshots. Her waist was sore from whining too much and her voice was hoarse from screaming over the loud music. The physical pain was nothing compared to the heartbreak she was experiencing over the shooting of Ray. She knew that Dolla was heartbroken. The only bright side to the evening was that she was home before her 9:30 curfew although Mercedes wasn’t there.

Envy learned two valuable lessons that night. Never get yourself caught up in someone else's drama and always trust your own instincts. Had Envy not obeyed her curfew, she would have been standing next to Dolla and Ray and there was no telling where the bullets would have landed.

Chapter 12

FRIENDS AGAIN

"Envy, you've been doing well since your punishment. Here is some money to add to what you've saved. Go buy you some school clothes so next week when school start, I don't want to hear nothing," Mercedes stated as she handed Envy $300.

"Thanks, Ma. You're the best, Mom," Envy stated as she kindly accepted the money.

"Yea, whatever. Whenever I'm giving you something, I'm the best mom, but when I'm disciplining yal, I'm a monster for a mother," Mercedes went on.

"No, Ma, it's not like that. You are always the best mom, but I just don't like to get in trouble for simple things that my other friends don't get in trouble for," Envy stated.

"Oh please, Envy. I'm a mother that cares and if you're not obeying my rules then you must be taught by the rod of correction. Check the BIBLE. It's okay to correct a child rather than allowing you to do as you please and going straight to hell," Mercedes lectured. "And that's why I Love you."

"How do you feel about me going to high school?" Envy asked.

"No, the question is how do you feel? Because I know what to teach you. I've gone through this phase in life, so I know what you're going to face and go against. It's on you to accept the lessons and follow what I'm teaching you," Mercedes stated.

"I'm cool about it. Actually, I feel good. I'm excited, and can't wait to meet the high school people. It's just that I don't know how they are going to treat me," Envy stated.

"Don't worry about them, worry about yourself, and the rest will come easy. You're no punk so you don't have to worry about the bullies. Pay attention, stay focused, and participate and you will pass your grades. Just don't get distracted by them lil stinking dangaling boys!" Mercedes warned and they both started laughing.

"Ma, how do you know they stank?"

"Because they do! Anyway, how do feel about Earl and Dre being here?" Mercedes changed the conversation.

"I love them! Dre gets on my nerves sometimes, but I'm used to them now. At first, I couldn't stand them. Well, not really Earl but Dre used to show off in front of Sylvia. Now they're cool. Are we keeping them forever?" Envy asked.

"I'm thinking about adoption, meaning keeping them, because their parents are not going to get it together, and I can't put these kids out like that. I love them too much," Mercedes stated.

"Then I'm all with it. Keep them," Envy agreed before asking, "Can I go to Centuries real quick?"

"Yes, go ahead and you better find somebody to go with you," Mercedes responded just as the phone began to ring.

Ring! Ring! Ring!

"Hello," Envy answered.

"Hello, Envy. So I guess you weren't going to call and check on me? Some friend you are!" India spoke sarcastically.

"Oh, what's up, India? You didn't call and check on me. I thought you had a problem," Envy snapped back.

"Well, I don't have a problem. You just get on my nerves sometimes but I still love you!" India confessed.

"Aww, I love you, toooo! Now come go with me to Century 21," Envy suggested.

"Okay, because I need to go school shopping, too," India responded before giggling.

"So you're using me, huh?"

"Oh well, I need you, too, so let's meet in front of the building," Envy stated and India agreed before meeting with one another only 10 minutes later.

"Aww, India, look how big Quandary is getting. She is too cute."

"I know, right? I promised my Aunt Maria that I would babysit today, so I'm bringing her with us," India stated.

"Okay, that's cool," Envy responded before they headed toward the train station.

As they were headed towards the train station, they ran into these grimy chicks from Roosevelt projects, some so-called bullies. One of the Roosevelt chicks bumped into India on purpose as they passed one another.

"Excuse you!" India quickly checked her.

"No tramp, excuse yourself!" the chick got fly about the mouth and you could feel the tension in the air.

"What, what you say?" India said, standing her ground.

"TRICK, YOU HEARD WHAT I SAID!"

"Whatever, you dirty bum! I don't have time for you," India responded, trying to brush it off.

"I will beat you senseless out here! What you wanna do?" the chick continued and it was on.

"Hold Qua for me, Envy," India stated as she handed Envy the baby.

Envy took hold of the baby and whispered, "And India, you better beat the brakes off of her!"

As soon as India handed over Qua, the chick punched her in the back of her head and it stung India. The girl landed two more blows before she and India got tangled up with one another. The girl swung India to the ground and was getting the best of her. Envy anxiously watched while holding the baby but also ensured that no one jumped in.

India managed to fight her way back to her feet and the girl backed up off of her. India was looking crazy and once she was back on her feet, she charged at the girl. It was quick but India had her by the hair and flung the chick to the ground and the tables had turned. India was punching the girl in the face with left and right blows when the crowd began to aggressively move closer and Envy stepped in between, "NAH! Hold up, HOLD UP… AIN'T NOBODY JUMPING IN! GET UP, INDIA," Envy spoke loudly and boldly as she used her free arm to pull India up.

India jumped up and kicked the girl in the stomach before realizing that her boobs were hanging out. Her hair was a mess and she was enraged as she tried to cover herself. The girl was getting up off the ground when an older guy walked over to defend Envy and India who were clearly outnumbered while holding a baby. He walked them to the train station and made sure they were okay before he left.

"Envy, why didn't you help me?" India blurted out while trying to fix her ripped shirt.

"How could I? How could I help you if I'm holding Qua?" Envy argued.

"What do you mean? My titties were hanging out and you're just standing there!" India angrily spoke.

"First of all, if it wasn't for me, they would've jumped you. That was a fair fight, no need for me to jump in. All I had to do is what I did, which is hold you down. At first, she got you, and then you got her. Nothing for me to do!" Envy stated in a tone of sarcasm.

"Whatever, Envy! I'm over it!" India stated as she rolled her eyes while fixing her hair.

"Whatever… You stay with an issue. Every time you look around, you're upset about something. You need to get over yourself," Envy stated.

During the ride, things were a little tense between the girls so the ride was quiet except for Qua wanting to be passed from arm to arm. The bums were walking through the trains begging for change with cups and people were singing and dancing for money as usual. It was like that until they reached the Broadway-Nassau and Fulton Street train station, the stop the girls had to get off at in order to get to Century 21.

The girls exited the train and remained quiet during the walk to Century 21. They spent the first 10 minutes browsing around the store as if they didn't know one another until India spotted something that she liked.

"Envy, look at these pants. Wouldn't they go nicely with a pair of Reeboks?"

"Yes, girl, those are hot! What are they, Moschino?" Envy asked.

"Yes. Look, they have more colors," India stated as she directed Envy toward the pants.

"OOOOUUU, look they have them in hot pink!!" Envy stated as she searched for her size. "If they have a size 28, I'm getting them!" she continued just as she grabbed a size 28.

"I like them, too. Envy, see if they have another size 28."

"Yep, they do. Here you go." Envy handed India the pants.

The girls searched for other items. Some were alike and some were different. After about 2 hours in Centuries, the girls were finally done. Outside of the shirt India purchased to change out the ripped one, they both bought about 7 or 8 high fashion, good quality outfits for no more than $250.00 (great discount). The girls then left the store.

"I'm hungry, Envy. Are you?" India asked.

"Yea, let's get some McDonald's."

"Okay, there it is right across the street, or do you want to eat inside the World Trade Center?" India asks.

"No, it's way too many people in there. Plus, it's too expensive! I'm good with McDonald's," Envy stated.

"Okay, come on then. That's cool," India stated.

The girls walked into McDonald's and ordered their food before sitting and eating.

"So, India, when did you start hanging out with Vikki?" Envy jumped right into it.

"She worked at my summer youth job, a grocery store in Flatbush," India stated.

"I can't stand her. She's always trying to start but she's a big punk."

"Yea, she told me that you and her got into it. Well, that you and Izel tried to jump her…"

"That chick is lying. Ain't nobody try to jump her. I did slap the taste out her mouth. Izel was just holding me down!" Envy interrupted.

"Well, like I told her. I don't have anything to do with it," India stated.

"You right. You don't have anything to do with it. But she is a liar. And really, you are my friend so in some form, you have everything to do with it because if it gets hectic, then what?" Envy asked.

"Well, that's a different story, but as far as now, there is nothing going on between yal. She and I ride the train together and do our lunch breaks together, so, therefore, whatever issue that yal have is irrelevant when we are at work. That's my point."

"Yea, you're right, but I still don't like her, and any minute it can go down!" Envy stated.

After the girls finished eating, they headed to the train station. This time, the ride was more comfortable because they bragged about what they brought from Centuries and how they would sport their new gear.

"I know what footwear I'm getting. I want some black on black suede Clark Wallabies," India stated.

"Ouuu, those would go well with the pink Moschino pants and the black Moschino shirt that we got. We can get off on Nostrand Ave and go to Murray's Corner (1 of the local sneaker stores)," Envy stated.

"Alright, but my knees are burning. When that chick made me hit the ground, I scraped my knee," India complained as she rubbed her right knee.

"That must've hurt because when you got up, man oh man, did you give her the business. I didn't think you had it in you. But you gave it up, and that's all that matters," Envy stated.

"Did you hear that bum broad talking about I'm sleeping with her man Stucky?" India asked. "Ugh, if Stucky ever messes with something like, that I will have jokes for days on him."

"Nostrand Avenue, next stop!" the train conductor's voice sounded off over the microphone.

The girls stood and prepared for their exit. A few minutes later, the train stopped and the girls got off and headed straight to Murray's corner.

"Damn, Fulton Street is as crowded as Manhattan," India stated.

"Yes, it is. We have to hurry up," Envy replied.

As the girls walked up Nostrand Ave, they ran into Envy's cousin Dora. "WHAT YAL DOING DOWN HERE?" Dora asked in her loud voice.

"We going to Murray's to get some Wallabies," Envy responded.

"What yal getting Wallabies for? And who baby yal got?" Dora asked while smiling at the cute little baby.

"Because we want them to go with our jeans, and this is India's little cousin," Envy responded.

"What type of jeans yal have?" she asked as she grilled both Envy and India from head to toe. Dora was always loud and said exactly how she felt. She stayed in an altercation with someone. She had the 'I don't give a damn' kind of an attitude. And at times, it could make her look really ugly.

"Why you look at me like that, Dora?" India asks.

"Because these are my eyes and I can look where I want," Dora sarcastically responded.

"Don't play with me, Dora!" India got feisty right back.

"No, don't play with me. You better get that thin looking ponytail out of my face," Dora responded.

"I'm not in your face, and first of all, you catching an attitude for no reason. I was just joking," India stated.

"WELL, DON'T PLAY WITH ME! I'M NOT A KID!" Dora continued being hostile.

"Okay, India, come on. It's getting late. We gotta go," Envy jumped in.

Envy and India headed their way and Dora went along her way. "Envy, you know that your cousin has a nasty attitude."

"Yes, she does," Envy interjected, not wanting India to bad talk her cousin. Envy knew that her cousin had a nasty attitude, but she was still her cousin.

The girls reached Murray's, copped their shoes and caught a cab back home.

"Okay, Mister, right here. Pull up in front of 671."

The cab driver did as he was directed and let the girls out after they paid him. Once they exited the cab, they said their goodbyes and headed home. When Envy got upstairs, Mercedes and the boys were eating dinner.

"JUST IN TIME!" Envy shouted as she opened the door with her key and a handful of bags. "Mmmm, Ma, what did you cook?"

"I made some pork chops, macaroni and cheese and corn."

"It smells good in here," Envy stated before taking her bags into her room, washing her hands and fixing her a plate. Even though she just ate in the city, there was nothing like a home cooked meal. Envy ate dinner, showered, and said her prayers before falling to sleep.

Chapter 13

BLOOD HAS BEEN DRAWN

The next day Envy and India had been hanging out on Malcolm X Boulevard all day and were tired by the time they arrived back on their block. They were headed toward Envy's building and talking when this tall, dark skinned guy with hazel eyes and a tattoo on his neck approached them out of nowhere.

"Hey, Chocolate! What's your name?"

"Why you wanna know my name? Who are you?" Envy sarcastically responded.

"You're a pretty chocolate girl and feisty. I like that. I wanna get to know you. By the way, my name is BK…Bloody King, I'm from Albany PJs. My sister recently moved in this building, so I'm new around here," BK stated.

"Well, my name is Envy and I'm from this building as well. Who is your sister?" Envy ask.

“Her name is Pamela but most people call her Ms. Pam. She lives on the second floor. And what’s up with you, Red? Why you so quiet?” he asked India.

“I’m just listening and observing,” India finally spoke.

“Oh, yes! I like, yal. Both of you are slick with the tongue. That’s sexy to me. I love a gangstress,” BK stated.

“I don’t know Ms. Pam, but I did see a new lady that live on the second floor. She’s short and dark skinned with locks in her hair? And what’s a gangstress?” Envy asked.

“Yea, that’s her. Short and dark with locks. And a gangstress is a female gangsta. A female that’s ready to bang anytime. A ride or die chick but carries herself like a lady. You know, a lady in the street but a freak in the bed,” he added.

“WOW! That’s a little too much for our young ears!” India shouted as she covered her ears.

“Yea, right. Yal know what I’m talking about. I know yal ain’t that pretty and sexy for nothing. AND yal bodies are fire!” BK complimented while rubbing his hands together with lust in his eyes.

All Envy could do was blush, excusing everything else that he said. All she heard were the compliments. "Thanks, BK, it was nice meeting you but we have to go," Envy spoke flirtatiously before exchanging a handshake with BK.

"But hold up, no number?" he asked as he held on to Envy's hand while trying to read her mood.

"What you mean?" Envy questioned before snatching her hand away.

"I mean I'm digging you. You're interesting and a brother wants to get to know more about you," BK continued, expressing his feelings.

"I'm sorry but I don't give out my number. But you'll see me around," Envy said, letting him know that she was no easy catch before she and India headed into the building.

"Okay, sexy! Next time we meet, I want that number," BK said confidently while watching the girl's backsides.

Envy and India kept walking as if they didn't hear him.

"Ugh, he seems really creepy," India expressed as they entered the building.

"Yes, he seems a little gay! What grown man has a perm, gold hair, and hazel contacts?" Envy joked and they both shrugged and chuckled at BK's appearance.

They took the elevator to the 5th floor and headed toward Envy's apartment. Before getting to Envy's apartment, they ran into Ms. Hunny, Kara's mother, on her way to the staircase.

"Hey, babies, where are yal going?" she spoke as they stopped momentarily in front of one another.

"Hey, Ms. Hunny, we're going to my apartment to chill. Where is Kara?" Envy asked.

"I don't know where Kara is but she better gets back around here soon," Ms. Hunny said quickly and kept on moving toward the staircase as if she was in a hurry.

Envy and India could hear voices in the staircase. "I guess it's a crack party going on," Envy mumbled out loud after hearing different voices laughing and giggling in the staircase.

They both shook their heads and Envy opened the door and the girls entered the apartment. After Envy slammed the door, someone quickly tapped on it before she could lock it.

"WHO IS IT?" Envy yelled with a frown on her face.

"It's me, Sylvia. Hey, Envy, can I get a piece of aluminum foil real quick? Please, please, please…"

Sylvia was feining and Envy knew how a crack fein was when they wanted to get high so she handed her the aluminum foil.

"Oh, don't tell your mom that I was here," Sylvia stated before hurrying back toward the staircase.

Envy knew that Mercedes told Sylvia not to come back until she got herself together and when she was ready to get her children back. However, Sylvia was in the building because it was around the 1st of the month and Ms. Hunny either borrowed money from Ms. Carroll or stole it.

Ms. Carroll was Kara's grandmother that took care of Kara being that Hunny was a serious addict and Kara's father died of AIDS years ago. Hunny knew that Kara received a check every 1st of the month from her father passing away. So Hunny would stay close by during the first few days of the month. After that, she would go on her crack binges for weeks at a time. Kara almost never saw her mom.

Sylvia and Hunny grew close when Sylvia first came to stay with Mercedes and from there, they'd been the best of buds. Almost like sisters. So even though Sylvia wasn't allowed at Mercedes' place, Ms. Carroll and family still welcomed her presence.

After Envy slammed the door, she rolled her eyes and expressed her feelings to India, "She's always sneaking over here knowing that my mother told her to stay away. She talking about don't tell? Watch, just as soon as my mother get here, I'm telling!"

They both laughed.

"You always telling. You're a snitch!" India joked.

"Well, then she needs to stop saying 'don't tell your mother' because my moms and I are seriously close. I basically tell her everything except for stuff that will get me in trouble."

The girls laughed as they flicked through the TV channels.

"Yea but I bet you won't tell your part. Oooo my God! Girl, what's this?" India excitedly expressed as her eyes focused on the TV, noticing a man and woman freaking off.

"I don't know. I didn't know that we had this channel. Jah must've ordered this," Envy spoke while blushing at what she was seeing.

"Let's watch it," India suggested.

"Ugh, India! Do you really watch stuff like this at your house?" Envy asked with her eyes still glued to the TV.

"Sometimes when my mother is not home. Her and my father have a whole collection."

"Is your father the short man?" Envy asked.

"Yes, that's my father," India answered.

"Then how did you come out looking Spanish if your mother is my complexion and your dad is my mom's complexion?" Envy inquired.

“I don’t know. Mostly because my grandmother from my dad side is Indian. She looks just like me,” India replied.

“Oh, okay,” Envy responded but really wasn’t buying that story.

India looked pure Spanish or Indian. Her mother was dark skinned and her dad was a dark caramel complexion with nappy hair. *Either that’s not her real dad or she’s adopted,* were Envy thoughts. India was an Indian complexion with pretty long hair and huge boobs like her mom. She looked like her mom, but their skin tones were very different. She was kind of thick for her age and about 5’5” tall.

As the girls continued to watch the porn, they began to feel how they were supposed to. Hot and horny!

“Envy, I’m getting horny. We gotta turn from this,” India mumbled out loud.

“Yes, girl, turn because watching this will have us out here doing some freaky things. When we are ready, we know what to watch to learn some moves and stuff,” Envy responded and they both burst out laughing. They then turned off the T.V and turned on the radio.

RING! RING! RING! RING!

"Hello," Envy answered.

"HELLO, ENVY! WHERE YOU AT? IT'S ME, PUG. DORA JUST GOT CUT."

"HUH? Wait a minute, Pug, and slow down. Where are you? Dora got cut where?" Envy frowned as she spoke before a knot of nervousness grew inside of her stomach.

Pug lowered his voice and calmly said, "I'm at St. John's Hospital. Dora's getting stitches right now. She got cut on the side of her face. One of them Blood girls cut her! They had a fight by Robeson."

"Okay, I'm on my way up there!" she said just before hanging up the phone. "Come on, India! I got to go. My cousin just got cut in her face!"

"Oh, my gosh! Do you need me to go with you?" India asked.

"Yea, come on." Envy quickly called a cab, wrote a note to her mother, informing her of what happened to Dora, and headed to the hospital.

The ride to the hospital was pretty quiet as Envy gently bit down on her bottom lip and deep thoughts.

Envy's thought, *I wonder which one of them bum broad's cut my cousin. How in the world did Dora get cut? I wonder where her friends were. Oh, these chicks are gonna get it!*

India was staring out of the window, dealing with her own thoughts. *That's messed up that Dora got cut but she probably ran off at the mouth to the wrong person. But damn, she's so young. I wonder how her face looks now. I know Envy wants to cry. What am I supposed to say or do? I hope the people that cut Dora is not at the hospital?*

"Okay, what side?" the cab driver asked after the five-minute ride to the hospital.

"Let us out in front of the emergency room."

The cab driver did as instructed. "Okay, six dolla."

Envy paid and the girls quickly exited the taxi. Once they entered the emergency room, Envy rushed over to the desk. "I'm looking for Dora Boswell," she spoke quickly to the clerk.

After a couple of seconds of the clerk browsing the computer for Dora's name, she informed Envy that Dora had just been discharged about 10 minutes ago.

"Okay, so what does that mean? Did she leave already?"

"Yes, she's gone. Once a patient is discharged, they leave immediately unless they are waiting for a ride, and they usually wait in that area right there to your left," the clerk explained as she pointed to a room behind the girls. "You can check in there and if you don't see her then she probably left already," the clerk continued.

"Okay, thank you," Envy replied as she and India rushed off to scan the waiting room.

There was no sign of Dora or any of Envy's family. Envy and India quickly rushed to St Marks, which is 4 shorts blocks away from the hospital. The girls walked so fast, you would think they ran.

By the time they got to the block, it was hot. Everyone was huddled up discussing what happened to Dora. Envy went straight into the building and upstairs to their 4th floor apartment.

"Hey, Aunt Bev, where is Dora?"

“Hey, Envy. Dora is in the room heavily senated (she meant sedated). I don’t think she’s in the mood for company,” Aunt Bev slurred.

“Well, I need to see her, aunty, so I’m going to wake her up,” Envy stated as she brushed past Aunt Bev to see Dora.

Dora was lying in her bed with her face all bandaged up, barely able to talk.

“Well, gone ‘head then. See if she gets up for you. Yal know how yal does,” Bev said with her country accent although Envy was gone already.

Envy sat down on the bed next to her and softly asked, “What happen to you, Dora?” Tears began to flow out of Envy’s eyes as Dora tried to answer.

“I don’t know,” Dora mumbled. “She…she cut me. She cut me,” Dora muttered as tears began to roll down her face.

“WHO, DORA!?” Envy shouted.

“She cut me, she cut…” Dora continued to repeat. Envy could barely hear Dora but was able to make out what she was trying to say.

"Okay, Dora. I'm gonna let you get some rest. I'll come back and visit you tomorrow," Envy stated as she hugged and kissed Dora, then left the room.

"HOLD ON, INDIA. I'M COMING. LET ME USE THE RESTROOM," Envy yelled from the back of the apartment, knowing that she really needed to get her cry out.

Seeing her cousin in this state was nerve wrecking and heart breaking. Envy knew that this was not going to be good for Dora and she felt every bit of her pain. Envy used the restroom, washed the tears off of her face and then exited.

"Okay, aunty. I'm going to go home now. I'll come back tomorrow to visit Dora," Envy painfully said.

Aunt Bev could hear the pain in her voice. She knew how close Envy and Dora were, so she knew that Envy was affected by seeing her like that. And it hurt Beverly to see her child cut up and her niece barely speaking because of a frog in her throat from trying to hold back her tears. This was a sad day for everyone close to Dora.

They left and Envy explained to India what happened and what Dora looked like. Once again, the ride home was quiet. All Envy could think about was almost losing her cousin.

Envy went back the next day to visit Dora. Dora told Envy that she had been cut by some Blood chick and of course, Envy knew that it was for sure beef. They just needed to wait for Dora to heal. Envy stayed at home waiting to hear the word from Dora because somebody had to pay for this!

TO BE CONTINUED!

47516611R00120

Made in the USA
Middletown, DE
27 August 2017